MR PEEL'S POSTERS

Jonathan Joy

MAPLE
PUBLISHERS

Mr. Peel's Posters

Author: Jonathan Joy

Copyright © Jonathan Joy (2021)

The right of Jonathan Joy to be identified as author of this work has been asserted by the author in accordance with section 77 and 78 of the Copyright, Designs and Patents Act 1988.

First Published in 2021

ISBN 978-1-914366-39-0 (Paperback)
978-1-915164-24-7 (Hardback)

Book Cover Design by: Jonathan Joy

Book layout by:
    White Magic Studios
    www.whitemagicstudios.co.uk

Published by:
    Maple Publishers
    1 Brunel Way,
    Slough,
    SL1 1FQ, UK
    www.maplepublishers.com

A CIP catalogue record for this title is available from the British Library.

All rights reserved. No part of this book may be reproduced or translated by any form or by any means, electronic or mechanical, including photocopying, recording or by any information storage and retrieval system without written permission from the author.

The views expressed in this work are solely those of the author and do not necessarily reflect the views of the publisher, and the publisher hereby disclaims any responsibility for them.

Disclaimer

Some of the items in Mr. Peel's Poster collection may be considered sensitive. While the collection may contain material that today may be considered prejudiced, stereotyped or offensive. It should be remembered that Mr. Peel's Posters are an important resource in the study of contemporary design and early nineteenth century London. The Posters published in this book are historical. They give an insight into a world of ideas, and interpretations that were very different from ours.

The author has taken all steps necessary to verify that the information is correct and assumes no responsibility or liability for any errors or omissions.

"My name is John Websdale Peel. I am a printer. I am a letter-press and copper-plate printer, and live in New-Cut, Lambeth. I am the son of the late John Peele of Duke Street, Lincoln Inn Fields. Tailor. I was never in prison in my life. I go to Ascot races; you may have seen me there – I kept a une deux cinq table. I promise to execute letter-press or copper plate cards in the first style of elegance, as also bills, circulars, &c, with the greatest despatch, or forfeit Five Pounds - For Self and Co. J, W. Peel, 9 Charlotte-terrace, New Cut, Lambeth. 1831. April 29th."

From Mr. Peel's own words. Written, Told, and Documented

CONTENTS

Chapter One – A Short History 8

Chapter Two – New Cut, Lambeth 16

Chapter Three – Apprenticeship 18

Chapter Four – Union Hall 20

Chapter Five – Mr. Peel and The Old Bailey 22

Chapter Six – Nero's Rescue 33

Chapter Seven – The Newspapers 35

Chapter Eight – Mr. Peel's PrintingOffice 37

Chapter Nine – The Steam Machine 40

Chapter Ten – Death 42

Chapter Eleven – The Probate Case 43

Chapter Twelve – Broadsheets 48

Chapter Thirteen – PermanentVenues – Astleys 53

Chapter Fourteen – Batty's 58

Chapter Fifteen – Cornwall's Royal Circus 61

Chapter Sixteen – The Royal Surrey Zoological Gardens 63

Chapter Seventeen – Vauxhall Gardens 65

Chapter Eighteen – The Victoria Theatre 68

Chapter Nineteen – Cremorne Gardens 70

Chapter Twenty – The Surrey Theatre 72

Chapter Twenty-One – The Grecian Saloon 74

Chapter Twenty-Two – Travelling Circuses-Clarkes 76

Chapter Twenty-Three – Cookes 78

Chapter Twenty-Four – Price and Powell's Circus 79

Chapter Twenty-Five – Exhibitions and Displays 83

Chapter Twenty-Six – Mr. Peel's Box Office 90

Chapter Twenty-Seven – Bridport Hall Prospectus 92

Chapter Twenty- Eight – Mr. Peel and the Wood Engravers 94

Chapter Twenty-Nine – Mr. Peel the Freemason 102

Chapter Thirty – Mr. Peel's Legacy 105

Acknowledgements 108

References 109

PREFACE

On 27th June 1914, Jessie Peel married my grandfather, Henry Joy. Jessie Peel was the great granddaughter of John Websdale Peele, 1794-1859.

Jessie Peel with her daughter Dorothy and son Kenneth Henry

The life of John Websdale Peele spanned a period in English history that brought great change to the lives of ordinary people. The Industrial Revolution. There was a vast movement of people away from the land. Away from rural towns and villages and into the ever-growing industrial cities. John Websdale's family were no exception. They had moved from Norwich, in rural Norfolk to London. London at the beginning of the nineteenth century was the largest city in Europe. Seat of government, it was growing at a phenomenal rate.

For some this was a time of extraordinary opportunity. This is the story of the life and work of one man who took that opportunity.

Archive research has given us back the life of John Websdale Peel, a forgotten figure in the creative development and production of typographic design and poster making. Wherever the archives make it possible, Mr. Peel, and those who knew him use their own words in the telling of his story.

PART ONE

MR. PEEL PRINTER. FORGET-IT-NOT
The Life of John Websdale Peel (1794-1859)

Chapter One – A Short History

The winter of 1794 was particularly severe. In Norwich, the excessive November rainfall had resulted in flooding of the lower parts of the city. By the time John Websdale Peele was born, in December of 1794, it was the cold thick frost that was overwhelming.

The summer of 1794 had been very different. May was warm, and the weather dry and sunny when 18- year- old John Peele, a tailor, married Frances Websdale at St. Peter Permountergate in Norwich, Norfolk. Since she was younger than him, it was customary for Frances's parents, William and Elizabeth to witness the wedding. Both signed the church register with their crosses.

John Peele and Frances Websdale's Marriage record:
at St Peter Parmentergate, Norwich. 25 May 1794

John Websdale Peele was their first born. Two years later Frances gave birth to a baby girl, Mary Ann. The baby sadly died in January 1797. A year later, another baby, a girl, also called Mary Ann was born. She survived. But the Norwich Church Registers also record the births and deaths of two more daughters: Emarantia on 10th November 1801 and Theressa Peel on 25th July 1805.

In August 1802, John Peel appears in the, United Grand Lodge of England Freemason Membership Registers, as aged 26, a tailor.

John Peele's entry in the, Norwich Moderns Grand Lodge Registers, 8th August 1802

Around 1810 John Peele takes the decision to leave Norwich and move to London, with his son, John Websdale, and his daughter Mary Ann. There is no mention of Frances from this time.

John Peele set up his tailoring business in Duke Street, Lincolns Inn, London. A note on the Apprentice Indenture for John Websdale Peele, dated 2nd February 1813, explains that his father John Peele, a tailor, had been living in Duke Street, Lincolns Inn, London, but was now deceased.

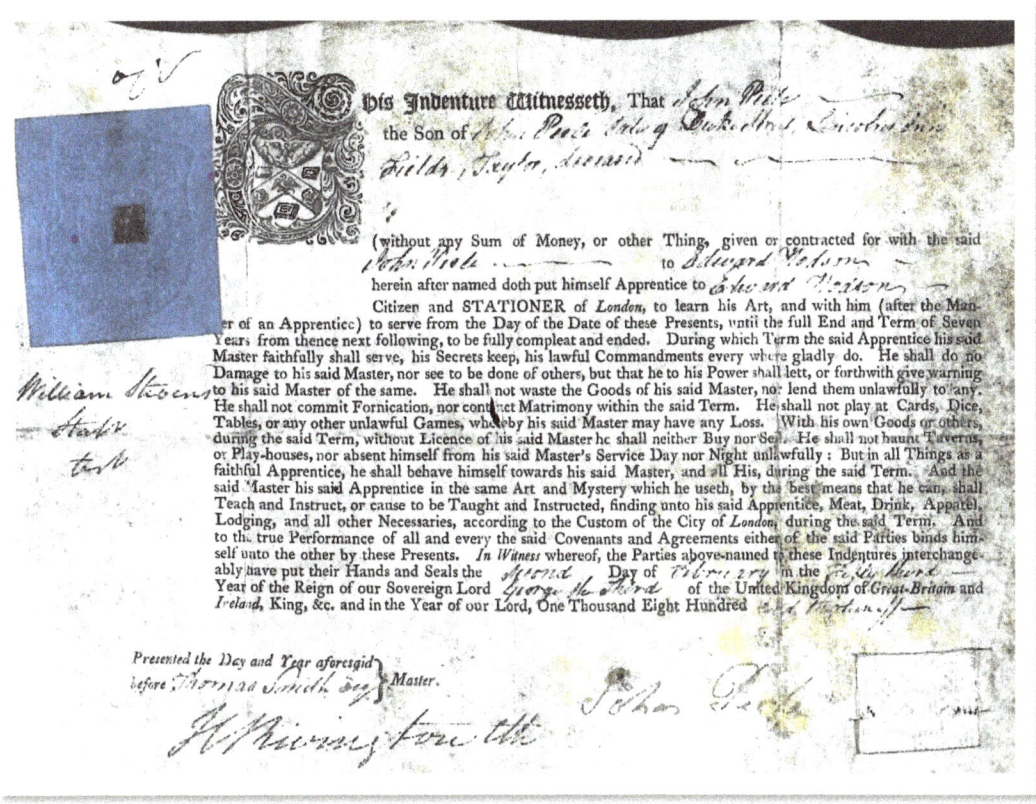

The Apprentice Indenture of John Websdale Peel, 2nd February 1813

In 1813 John Websdale Peele had become an apprentice to Edward Hodson, Printer of Cross Street, Hatton Garden. All went well until four years into his apprenticeship. When on Sunday 14 September 1817 Edward Hodson died suddenly. There is nothing to indicate whether John Websdale's apprenticeship was completed at the Hodson's printing works. It is equally probable that he may have completed his apprenticeship under the watchful eye of William Stevens, a master printer. For it is his name that appears to the side of the original iIndenture, beneath the seal.

In November 1819 he took time off to be a witness at his sister Mary's wedding to Richard Grayden of Lambeth, a very successful brush maker. After seven years, in 1820, John Websdale Peele, also known as Jem or Jemmy, completed his apprenticeship.

It was not until the year 1829 that he dropped the final 'e' in his surname.

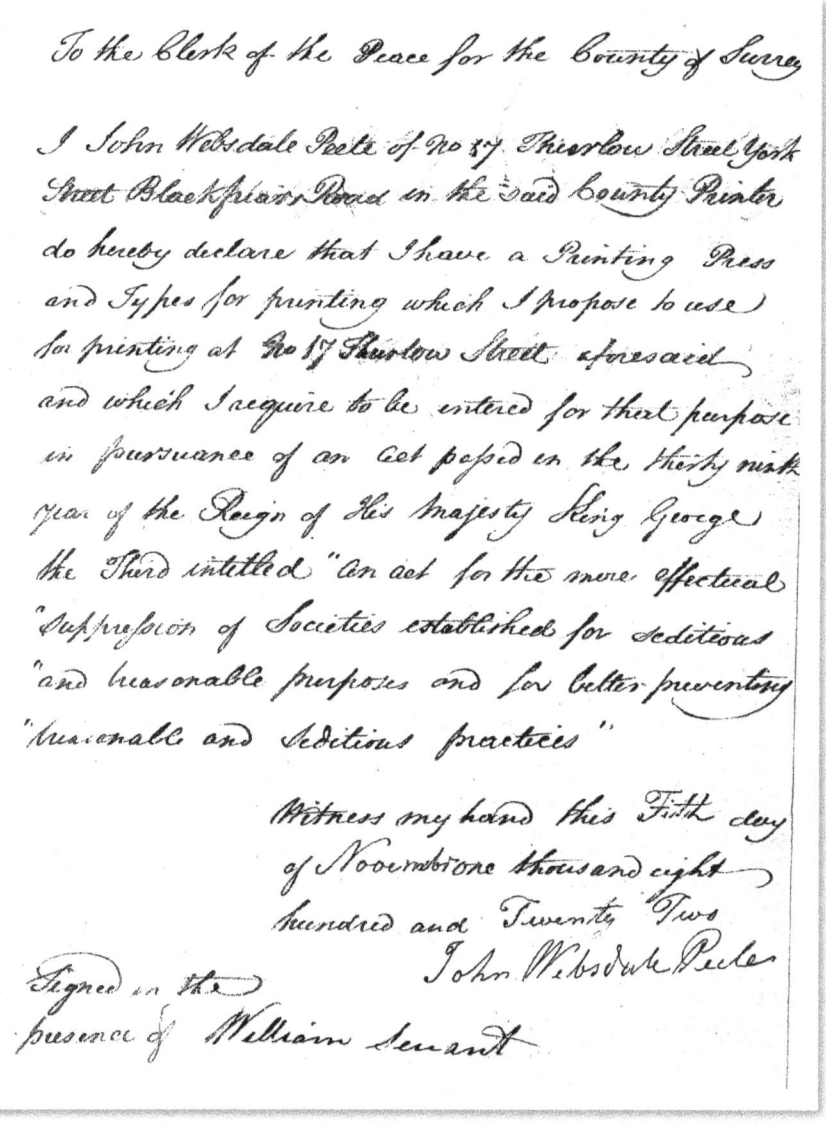

Notice of Printing Press Mr. Peel, 5th November 1822

Bonfire Night, the 5th November 1822, and John Websdale applied to the Clerk of the Peace for the county of Surrey to operate a printing press at 17 Thurlow Street York Street, Blackfriars Road, London. York Street was very close to Charlotte Street, Charlotte Terrace and New Cut, where from 1823 John Websdale Peel would live, work and spend the rest of his life.

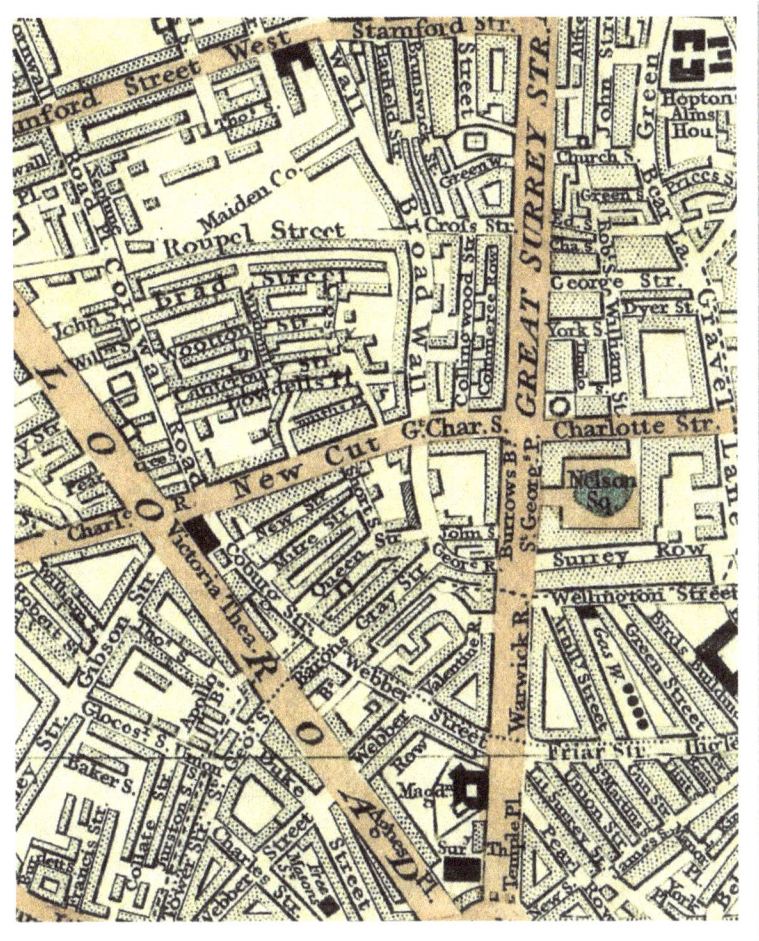

New Cut, Lambeth from Cary's New Plan of London 1837

New Cut, Lambeth from Pierce Egan's Life in London, 1821

On 11 February 1827 John Websdale Peele married Sophia Neven at her local parish church, St George in the East, London. Sophia proved a perfect partner for John. As he explained to the Old Bailey Court in June 1831 "...my wife was at home – she works in the business, and saw the defendant; I believe she was in the kitchen – she was about the premises; I cannot say whether she was in the office or not, but she saw him – she was backwards and forwards..."

Marriage Record, Mr. Peel and Sophia Neven. St George in the East

Sophia herself remembers, "... I cannot tell the date on which he first came... we had dined; Barber dines with us – I think we had dined, but I do not recollect such a trifling circumstance; as near as I can recollect we had dined – I am confident he did not come so early as one o'clock; the apprentice was in the office, and so was I part of the time – I cannot say how long I staid; there was nobody else in the lower office Barber was at work; I do not remember whether the presses were going – I paid no attention to the conversation between my husband and the defendant; I was in the office in which the presses were – my husband and Hayley were in a small place, a sort of counting-house; it is not a regular counting-house, but only some boards placed across – it is one room; I do not think anybody else was at work in the office..."

Two years on, and life at No. 9 New Cut was very different. By early 1834 Sophia had left; setting up with William Stevens. They both applied for a licence to use a printing press and types at No.11 Cornwall Road on 29th May 1837.

Another two years and the England & Wales Civil Registration Death Index for 1839 records the death of Sophia Peel during the third quarter of that year.

Early 1834 and John Websdale Peel was living with Cecilia Stapleton and her son George. A trusted apprentice, George Stapleton would eventually become a master printer himself. On October

14th 1834, Cecilia gave birth to a son, John Peel. Two years later, almost to the day, she gave birth to a daughter, Cecilia Stapleton Peel. In 1848, a third child, Theresa Jane Peel was born.

This was to prove a very productive period for Mr. Peel's printing business. The early work of advertisements, broadsides and broadsheets gave way to the more profitable Theatre and Circus posters. Living and working at No.9 New Cut, John Websdale was four doors away from George Bolwell Davidge at no.5 Charlotte Terrace, New Cut. Davidge was Actor / Manager of The Coburg Theatre, opposite, for seven years – 1826 to 1833. On 15th April 1831, John Websdale had signed Davidge's application for a printing press at the Coburg; and in 1833 he printed a poster for the Royal Victoria Theatre (late Coburg). It is no surprise that Mr. Peel and Mr. Davidge got on well, as Davidge was originally apprenticed to a printer.

 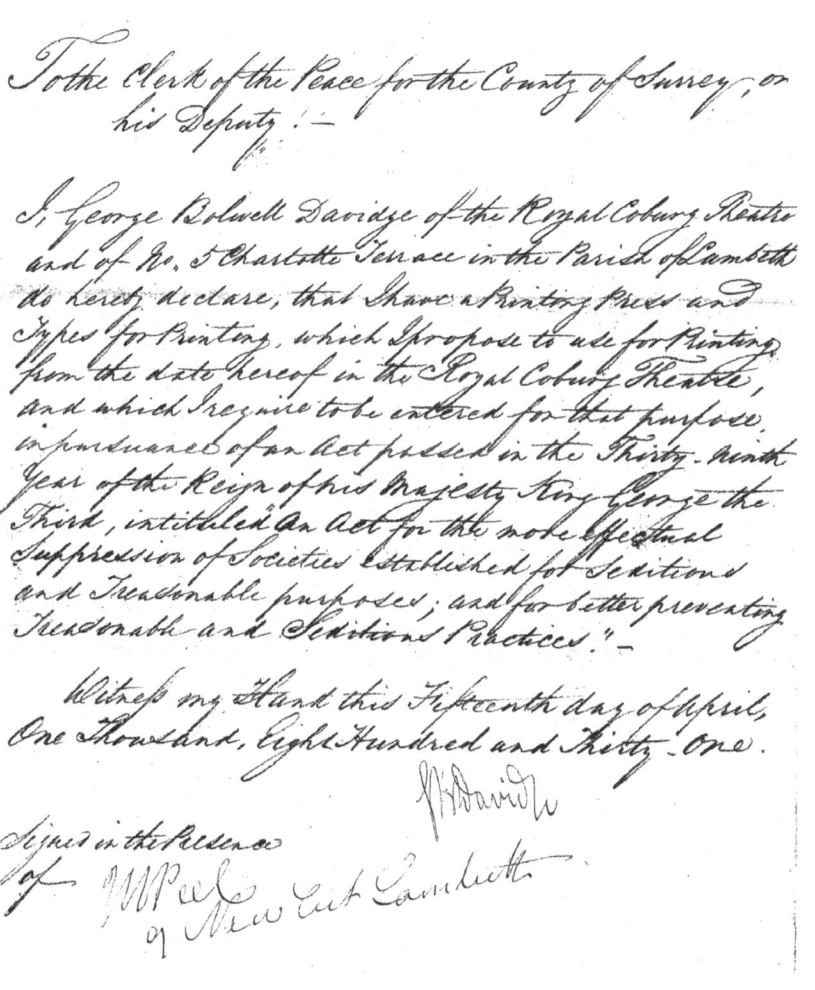

George Bolwell Davidge (1793-1842)   *Notice of Printing Press, The Royal Coburg Theatre, 1831*

On 31 January 1842 in Davidge Terrace, Walcot Place, Lambeth, George Bolwell Davidge died. He was in his 50th year and thought to have been worth at least £27,000 when he died. His will contained numerous generous legacies.

Given Mr. Peel's close theatre and circus ties, the business was soon producing promotional material and posters for such venues as Astleys, Batty's Circus & Olympic Arena, and Cornwall's Royal Circus.

In 1847, John Websdale Peel appears to suffer from an illness that sets him back. Charles Smith remarks on it at the Old Bailey in April of that year "... he told me Mr. Peel was very poorly...". One year later and it is Cecilia Stapleton who is signing the Printing Press Licence application.

Mr. Peel recovered short-term, but the illness had taken its toll. John Henry Marr, a compositor in the service of J W Peel for sixteen years, told the Court of Common Pleas on November 28th 1860: "Mr. Peel had a wife, but she is not living with him, nor was there during part of 1856 a soul in the house." Marr goes on to explain that a Mrs. McNabb was, in his opinion, employed at 74 New Cut in 1857 "...more as a nurse than a servant."

Mrs. McNabb herself recalled. "He was an invalid both in his hand and feet....Mr.Peel was an irritable man, but we did not fight; there was nothing more than words."

Charles W Herbert who had worked for J. W. Peel as a traveller also stated to the Court. "They all used to get drunk. She (Mrs. McNabb) very often got drunk. Mr. Peel and she were in the habit of quarrelling, and that he, (Mr. Herbert) had to come between them, so had Mr. Peel's daughter."

Cecilia his daughter said she left to get married, but that she went back a few days before Mr. Peel's death. Mr. Peel died on 6th December 1859. "The day Mr. Peel died Mrs. McNabb lay on the hearth-rug in front of the fire quite drunk, and Mr. Edmonds, the doctor, had to step over her to get to Mr. Peel."

Mr. Peel's Death Certificate 6th December 1859

John Websdale Peel's Death Certificate records the cause of death: Jaundice with disease of Liver and Kidneys Certified.

Five years after Mr. Peel's death. A poster was printed that stands as a testament to the influence and high regard with which John Websdale Peel was remembered. It simply reads:

CREMORNE Wednesday July 20th 1864 GODARDS GRAND ASCENT One Shilling

Printed by Nowell's (late Peel's) Steam Machine, 74 New Cut, Lambeth.

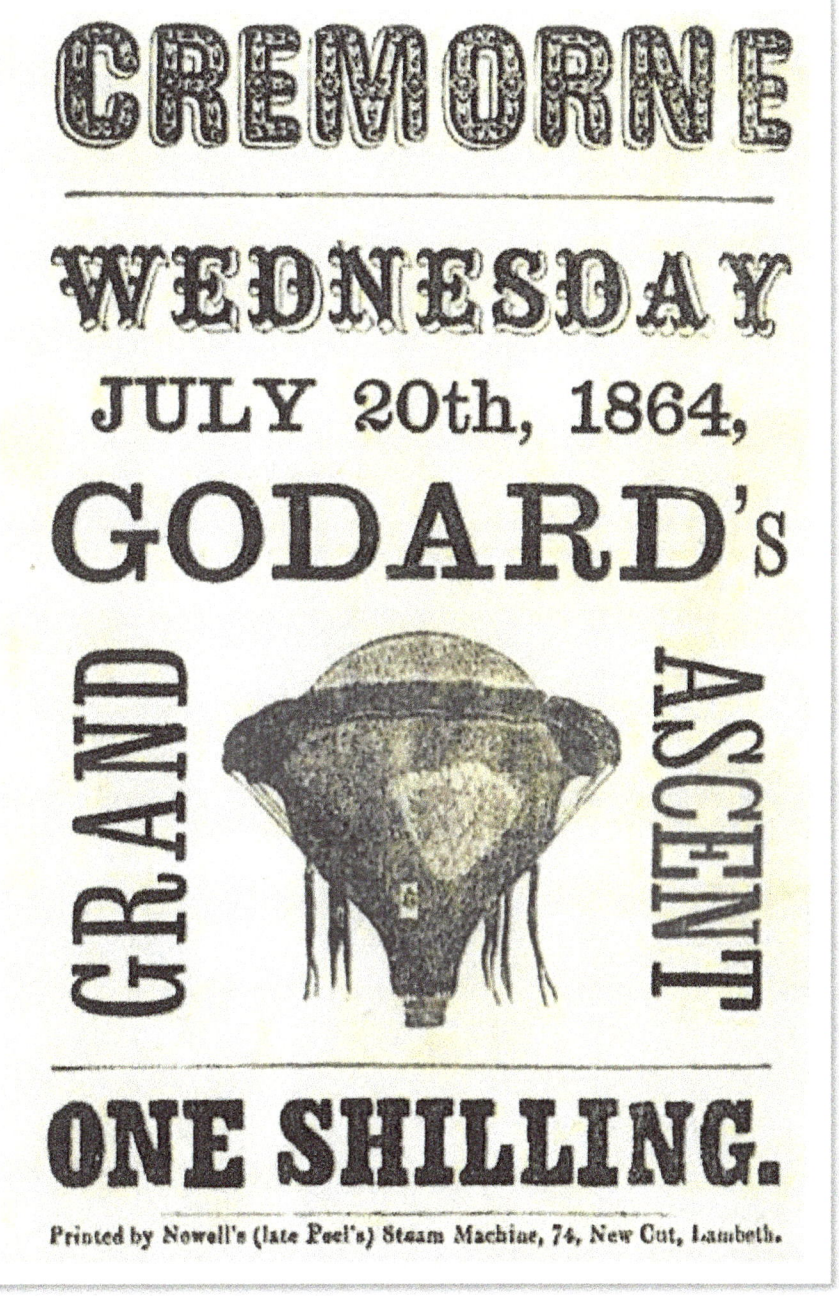

Poster for Godard's Grand Ascent, Cremorne, 1864

Chapter Two – New Cut, Lambeth

There is a street in London which runs between Waterloo Road in Lambeth and Blackfriars Road in Southwark. It is perhaps best known as being the location of the well-established Old Vic theatre at the western (Lambeth) end, as well as the more experimental Young Vic theatre at number 66, halfway along on the other side. It is called The Cut (formerly New Cut).

On Sunday 14th January 1872 The Observer carried an article – THE NEW CUT ON SUNDAY MORNING it read; "... by far the largest, as well as the best known of these Sunday markets or fairs, is that held in Lambeth Lower Marsh, generally known as the " New Cut."

New Cut, Lambeth 1870

What first strikes the sightseer bound on a visit to the New Cut Market is its remarkable isolation within the thoroughfare in which it is held…it is concentrated wholly within its own precincts. As one journeys toward it down the Waterloo Road, the Sunday morning quietude of that thoroughfare is unbroken as far as the South Western station. Nearer the Cut there are a few groups of gossipers, a shop or two standing open, and an old lady in yellow leggings seated on a doorstep, and offering fuses (matches) for sale…. at the Victoria Theatre the bank of humanity stands up like a barricade, and right and left stretches the market, with its swarm of customers and loungers…

There is no classification in the gutter-market. A vegetable barrow is located between a stand on which old iron is exposed and another where a quack doctor with infinite gag is disposing of his pills and potions. The barrows and stands are ranged by the kerb stones; about one half of the shops are open; iIn front of many of those closed there are stands, where hats and caps are on sale; on the pavement between, and in the open centre of the road, the throng slowly and somewhat spasmodically circulates…

The London working man – the genuine working man, the labourer, the scavenger, the coal whipper, the dustman, representatives, indeed, of all kinds of unskilled and poorly paid labour, are here in great force, lurching to and fro unwashed, dressed in their working clothes, unshorn, unbootblacked, and generally unlovely, but no ruffians for all that… these men meet each other here once in a week, and give one to another that gruff, not unkindly salutation… two big rough, easeze-clad men meet and grunt. "Morning" one to another. They walk some ten paces in abstracted silence. At length one ponderously asks of the other, "How's little Tommy?" "Better" is the laconic response, and another interval of silence succeeds. "Has Dick ever stumped up that 'ere three bob he owed you?" "No, and the begger has hooked it (gone)." "Well, morning Bill." "Morning Jem." And so the two friends part…

John Websdale Peel, whose nickname also happened to be Jem, lived and worked at three addresses during his time in New Cut. From 1823 – 1829 he was at 31 New Cut, Lambeth. Then from 1829 – 1838 he lived at 9 Charlotte Terrace, New Cut; And from 1838 – 1859 he occupied 74 Charlotte Terrace, New Cut, Lambeth.

On the Sixth February 1846 John Websdale Peel serves notice that he has a printing press and types at 19 Little Windmill Street, New Cut, Lambeth. This appears to be a property very near 74 Charlotte Terrace, New Cut. In fact when the document is signed, someone starts to write 74 New Cut. An adjoining property would have its advantages at this time: not only another press, but more space for storage,; such as Paper, printed or blank; Compositors type-cases; Wood letter poster type; Metal type – lead, antimony for casting; – hand setting equipment, the inks, and rollers and inking balls. Guillotines, stitchers, binders, and booklet-makers. Not forgetting the solvents that were necessary for cleaning up after printing.

Chapter Three – Apprenticeship

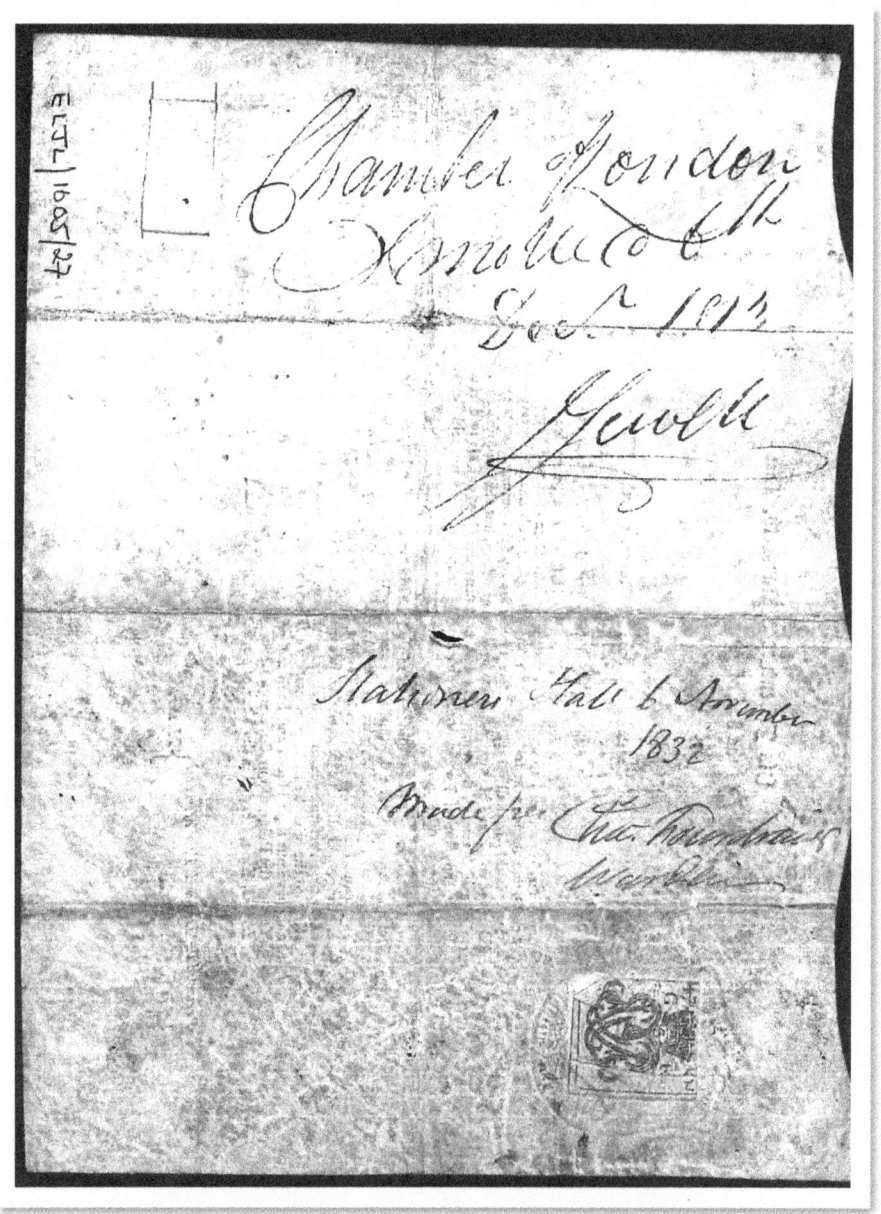

Fourteen. J. W. Peel's Apprenticeship Indenture. 1813

The apprenticeship indenture was a legal document required by anyone who wished to enter a trade professionally, meaning that no one could work as a master of the craft until they had served their full apprenticeship period. Typically this period was at least seven years long.

In 1813 John Websdale Peele had become an apprentice to Edward Hodson, Printer of Cross Street Hatton Garden. As an apprentice he was a Printer's errand boy. In a printing establishment, he would have performed a number of tasks, such as mixing tubs of ink, and fetching and making type. The practice of apprenticeship transferred children or adolescents to an interim household, for a set period of time. In John Websdale's case, seven years.

In theory an apprentice needed no payment or wage, the technical training provided in return for the labour given. However, it was usual to pay the apprentice a small sum. This would buy new clothes and other necessaries. All apprentices learned more than practical skills and the meaning of hard work. They also were expected to abide by rules of moral and professional behaviour. As teacher and role model, the master served a public function. One from which the whole community benefited.

All went well for four years into his apprenticeship. Then on Sunday 14 September 1817, Edward Hodson suddenly died.

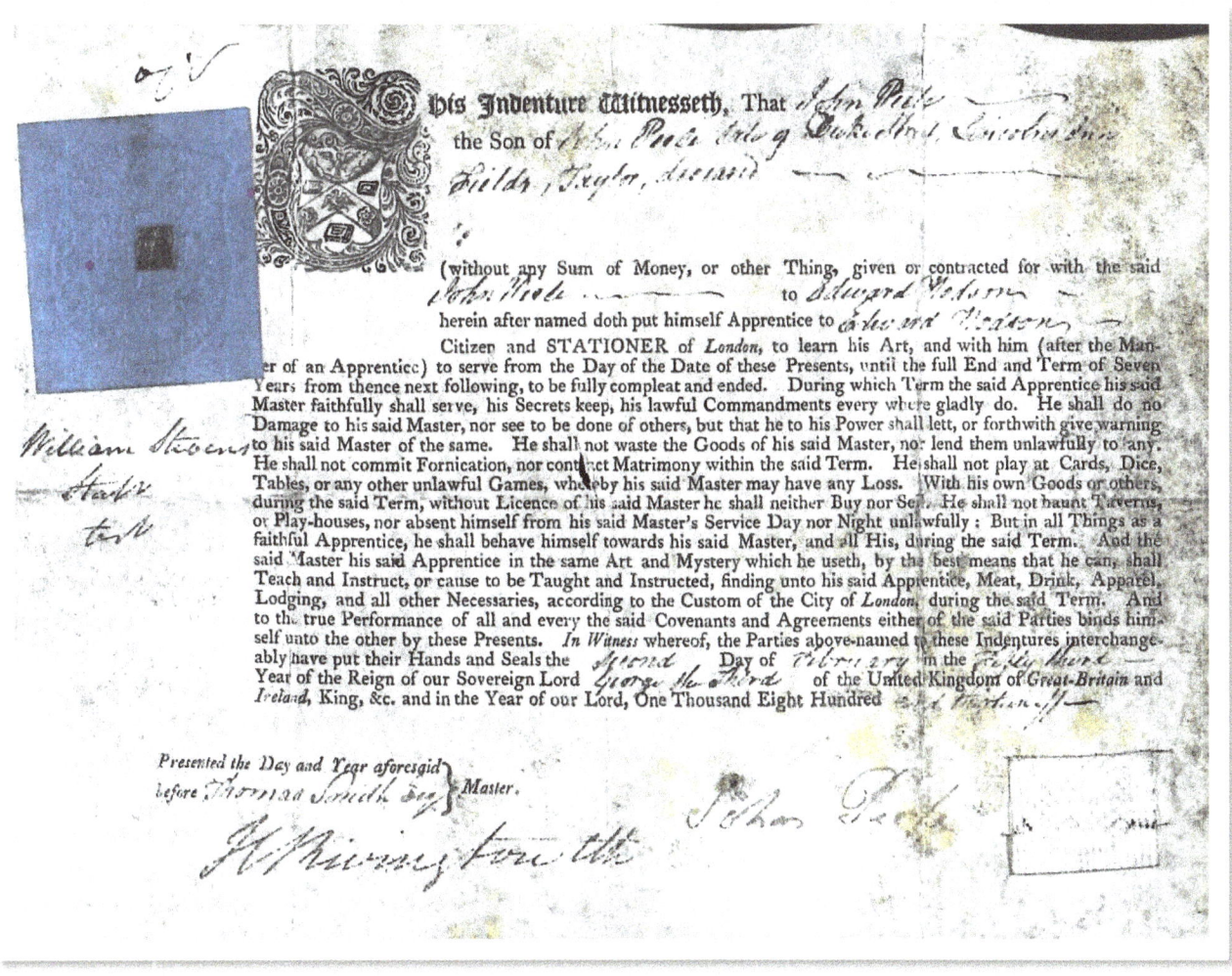

Chapter Four – Union Hall

Having completed his apprenticeship John Websdale Peele set up a printing press at 17 Thurlow Street York Street, Blackfriars Road, London. York Street was close to Charlotte Street, Charlotte Terrace and New Cut, where from 1823 John Websdale Peele would live, work and spend the rest of his life.

Under the Unlawful Societies Act of 1799 every person having a printing press or types for printing and every person making types or printing presses had to deliver a signed notice of this to the clerk of the peace, who was to file such notices and transmit attested copies to the Secretary of State.

The Act continued:

"And be it further enacted, that every Person who shall sell Types for Printing, or Printing Presses, as aforesaid, shall keep a fair Account in Writing of all Persons to whom any such Types or Presses shall be sold, and shall produce such Accounts to any Justice of the Peace who shall require the same; and if such Person shall neglect to keep such Account, or shall refuse to produce the same to any such Justice, on Demand in Writing to inspect the same, such Person shall forfeit and lose, for such Offence, the Sum of Twenty Pounds."

For the most part of his life as a Master Printer, John Websdale Peel conformed to this Act, many of the Notices of Printing Presses in Surrey 1822-1858 given by John Websdale Peel survive.

> Mr. Adolphus then retired.
> UNION-HALL.—John Websdale Peele a pri[nter] in the New-cut, Lambeth, was summoned on a[n information] charging him with being the publisher of nine pape[rs, the] matter of the most improper description, without [either] either his name or place of abode, contrary to an [Act of] the 39th year of the reign of George III., entitled [an Act for] the more effectual suppression of societies establis[hed for sedi]tious and treasonable purposes, and for better preve[nting season]able and seditions practices," whereby he had bec[ome liable to] pay the sum of 20l. for each of the nine papers, mak[ing] the sum of 180l. in the event of a conviction.
> The clerk having read the information setting for[th the nature] of the offence, the defendant pleaded "not guilty."
> The case was fully proved.
> The Magistrates, who were very much incline[d to] convict on the nine cases, at the request of the L[earned Counsel] inflicted two penalties of 20l. each on the defendant.

London Courier & Evening Gazette. 2nd July 1830

There is however a newspaper report that gives another side to Mr. Peel's activities.

Recording the proceedings at Union Hall; The Surrey Magistrates Court, which served a district covering a large part of South London including Lambeth and Southwark, was the

LONDON COURIER AND EVENING GAZETTE. Friday 2 July 1830

UNION-HALL, John Websdale Peele, printer, residing in the New-cut, Lambeth, was summoned on information charging him with being the publisher of nine papers, containing matter of the most improper description, without adfixing either his name or place of abode, contrary to an Act passed in the 39th year of the reign of George 111, entitled "An Act for the more effectual suppression of societies established for seditious and treasonable purposes, and for better preventing treasonable and seditious practices," whereby he become liable to pay the sum of £20. For each of the nine papers, making together the sum of £180. In the event of conviction.

The clerk having read the information setting forth the nature of the offence, the defendant pleaded not guilty."

The case was fully proved.

The Magistrates, who were very much inclined at first to convict on the nine cases, at the request of the Learned Counsel inflicted two penalties of £20. Each on the defendant.

This verdict is later mentioned by Mr. Peel himself, and Isaac Latimer, an apprentice to Mr. Peel, in the Proceedings of the trial of William Hayley at The Old Bailey on 30th June 1831.

Chapter Five – Mr. Peel and The Old Bailey

The Proceedings contain accounts of trials which took place at the Criminal Court of the Old Bailey. At the same time, accounts of what happened at the Old Bailey were reported in increasing detail in the newspapers. These records show that between 1825 and 1847, John Websdale Peel made at least six visits to the Old Bailey.

Old Bailey and Newgate gaol

The first was as a witness in the trial of JAMES EASTON, for Theft – pocketpicking and JOHN CLARK, Theft- pocketpicking, 13th January 1825. JAMES EASTON and JOHN CLARK were indicted for stealing, on the 8th of December, a handkerchief, value 2 s., the goods of Thomas Boyes, from his person. JOHN WELSDALE PEEL- "I am a printer. I was passing, and saw a mob – Mr. Boyes had a handkerchief in his hand, and said he had taken it from Easton's small clothes. I saw Boston take Clark, who put himself in a fighting attitude, Easton ran from Mr. Boyes, but was taken afterward.

Verdict Guilty; EASTON – GUILTY . Aged 19. Confined Two Months and Whipped. CLARK – GUILTY . Aged 34. Transported for Life.

The next time John Websdale Peel appeared at The Old Bailey was on the 30th June 1831. Both he and his wife Sophia gave evidence in the trial of WILLIAM HAYLEY who was accused of Deception and Fraud. This complicated trial involved the forging and printing of bogus Share Certificates in the Potosi La Paz, and Peruvian Mining Association…

JOHN WEBSDALE PEEL - . "I am a letter-press and copperplate printer, and live in the New-cut, Lambeth. I have known the defendant about two years; when I first knew him he gave the name of Smith. In March last, when I came home one day, I found him at my house – my young man had taken an order from him, and entered it in the name of Spicer and Co. - the prisoner then ordered me to engrave a plate like a copy which he had got – (looking at a share) it was as near like this as the engraver could do it; he said the former plate was lost, that Mr. Ellis, the engraver, had offended the gentlemen, and there would be a great many other things to be done – I was to engrave this as quick as I could; it had the name of Ellis, as the engraver, and was dated 1827 – I said it was copper-plate; he said Yes, but the plate was lost, and I was to do another; I got one engraved – a proof was thrown off, which I showed to him on paper at my house; he ordered one hundred to be engraved on parchment – I gave the plate, the whole hundred engravings, and the original they were copied from, all over to the defendant – I was paid 7l. for my trouble; I gave a receipt for the money, in the name of Spicer and Co., and delivered it to the defendant, as my young man entered the work to be done in that name – he made not the least objection to the receipt being in that name – (looking at nineteen impressions) I have no doubt these are all impressed from the same plate."

Cross-examined by MR. ALLEY.. Q. Have you been a speculator in these shares at all? A. No; I never saw Mr. Measam till about May, nor did my wife, to my knowledge – I was taken into custody about these plates; it was then I saw Mr. Measam – I was in custody four or five days till I could find the defendant; I was not in prison, but in a lock-up house at night, and went out with the officer in the day-time to find him – I was never in prison in my life; I was at the office about disposing of indecent prints, and paid the £20. Penalty for it – one of my apprentices was a witness against me; I have not been in trouble about anything else – I go to Ascot races; you may have seen me there – I kept a '"une deux cinq' table,;" I never said Mr. Measam employed me to engrave these shares - Barker, who superintends my business when I am out, was present when the defendant came; I did not say, at Unionhall, that nobody was present – he had spoken to Barber, but when I came in and took the business Barber left, and was at a little distance in the office when I took the order.

Q. In the same room?

A. No, the office is divided – there are two rooms, the press and composing-rooms; he left me with Mr. Hayley – he might have heard our conversation if he had paid attention to it; I do not know whether he did; he might have heard part of it – my wife was at home – she works in the business, and saw the defendant; I believe she was in the kitchen – she was about the premises; I cannot say whether she was in the office or not, but she saw him – she was backwards and forwards; he was dressed in a very dark olive or black surtout coat, and wore glasses – I do not know anything about Mr. Measam...

CHARLES FREDERICK BARBE:. I am journeyman to Mr. Peel. I first saw the defendant in March last – he came to the office to have a plate engraved for the Potosi Association; Mr. Peel was not at home when he came in - he showed me a copy on parchment, similar to this (looking at one); I declined giving him an estimate of the price till Mr. Peel came in, as I did not know the price of engraving – I asked if he would leave his name; he gave me Spicer and Co.; our office is in the back premises below, and as I was shewing him upstairs, I met master – the conversation between them was not exactly in my hearing, for the office where we work has a deal of bustle in it; I did not bear what passed – I saw him leave in about ten minutes; as far as I can recollect, he wore a frock coat, and wore glasses – I saw him again four or five days after, when he came to our house to see a proof of the plate; I was not present when it was shown to him, nor did he say anything to me about it – I know the engraving had been done then; I saw him again on the Saturday in the same week, when he came to fetch them away – I think it was the same day as he saw the proof; he took away the impressions, which were on parchment, the plate, and the copy it was engraved from – I did not see him pay anything, and did not see him again till he was apprehended; I am quite sure he is the person.

Cross-examined by MR. PHILLIPS. Q. Can you give us the day of the week that he first came? A. No – I know it was Saturday that he saw the proof, as there was a chimney on fire opposite; I cannot say which house – I have no other reason – it was about four or five o'clock; I have lived with Peel about nine months – I did not notice the colour of the defendant's glasses; he had a dark coat, inclining to brown – I know his features, but did not examine him all over; I cannot say what cravat he wore – there were two more men at work in the office, about four yards from master, but you cannot hear while the press is going what persons in the counting-house are talking of, unless you chose to be inquisitive and listen; I cannot say how long these men had been in master's employ, nor recollect their names – they merely came to work a job off; there is a small partition to the counting-house, but still they might see the defendant – he did not pass them to go out; I did not ask the defendant where he lived, but it was asked, because I was desired to put down Stangate – I have the book here: I asked Mr. Peel if he had left his address – he said Stangate; master said he had told him where he lived – if he has said he did not ask him, he must have said an untruth to me, or to the gentleman who asked him, if he did.: Mrs. Peel was going backwards and forwards in the office – I cannot say how near she was to him; she passed him, I believe – as far as I can recollect this was in the morning; it might be ten o'clock, or it might be three – the order was given and executed in March, but I cannot tell the day of the month.

MR. ADOLPHUS. Q. Were the two men in the office at press or composing? A. They were at press that day; it makes a great noise, and engages their attention – the counting-house is separated by a partition: the men were not in our constant employ – I saw the defendant at Unionhall, and had a doubt of him till I heard him speak, on account of his not having spectacles, but had not the least doubt then, and have none now.

SOPHIA PEEL: . I am the wife of Mr. Peel. I saw the defendant at our house in March last, several times in in that month, and I had seen him about two years ago – he then left us the name of Smith; we then lived further up, in the same street – he came to have some printing done; I did not see him again till last March, and recognized him as the person I had seen – he came to know if my husband could engrave a plate for him, and brought a proof with him; Mr. Peel not being at home, he asked Barber if Mr. Peel could engrave a plate like that copy; he told him Yes – I saw the copy he produced; it was like this and printed on parchment – Mr. Peel met him as he was going out, in the passage; I afterwards saw him when he came to see a proof of the plate – I told him it was not ready then, and he was to come on Saturday; I know that he came on Saturday, and waited a quarter of an hour till Mr. Peel came in – I sent our lad for the proof; I took the proof from the lad who brought it, and Mr. Peel came in – I gave it to him, and he showed it to the defendant; I saw him when he came the same night and took them away – I put them up in the kitchen, and just as Mr. Peel came to the door the defendant came in and had them; my husband was taken to Union-hall on this charge, and detained six days – while he was detained I went out, by direction of the Magistrate, with ease, the officer, to find the defendant; I went to the Royal Exchange, and several places – I at last stationed myself on London bridge, and while there the defendant passed; I pointed him out to ease, and said I was confident in my mind he was the man, but I would not swear to him till I saw him full in the face – I went up, and spoke to him; directly he saw me he put his handkerchief up to his face – I asked if his name was Thompson, or Thomas – I hardly know which, I was in such a state of agitation; it was the first name that came to my mind – he told me that was not his name; I said my name was Peel, and asked if he did not know me – he said no, he did not, he had no knowledge of me whatever; I said I was confident he did know me, for Mr. Peel had done some work for him – he said no, he did not know me, but when he first saw me he thought me very much like a servant that lived with him; I left him, and went to speak to ease – I told him I had not had a sufficient view of his countenance, but we would watch him, see where he went to, and Mr. Peel should come and see him; we followed him up Gracechurch-street – he went up and down several courts, and when he got to the corner of Bishopsgate-street he looked round to see if I was following him; he had looked round several times before, and not wishing him to see me I went into a shop; when I came out both him and ease were gone – I saw him before the Magistrate the same afternoon; I am confident he is the person, for I answered the door every time to him.

Cross-examined by MR. PHILLIPS. Q. You answered the door the first time, and all? A. Yes – I think it was three times; it was not to me he spoke about the engraving – he asked me if Mr. Peel was at home; I asked him down to Barber – I cannot tell the date on which he first came; I rather think it was the beginning of March, and I think between three and four o'clock – we had dined; Barber dines with us – I think we had dined, but I do not recollect such a trifling circumstance; as near as I can recollect we had dined – I am confident he did not come so early as one o'clock; the apprentice was in the office, and so was I part of the time – I cannot say how long I staid; there was nobody else in the lower office -Barber was at work; I do not remember whether the presses were going – I paid no attention to the conversation between my husband and the defendant; I was in the office in which the presses were – my husband and Hayley were in a small place, a sort of counting-house; it is not a regular counting-house, but only some boards placed across – it is one room; I do not think anybody else was at work in the office.

Q. How came you to call the defendant Thomas? A. I had asked the officer what I should do to see his face, but he kept his handkerchief up over his nose and mouth all the time – I do not think anybody was at work at the presses when he was there, but I am in and out so many times I do not take notice; sometimes we are busy. And take extra men – my husband was once taken to Unionhall through a person informing against him; his apprentice's indentures were cancelled – I was never taken up; - yes, I was, at Union-hall.

MR. BODKIN. Q. Do you mean that an officer took you into custody, or were you desired by any writing to go to Union-hall? A. I never was taken up by an officer anywhere; a man had come into the house after this trouble of Mr. Peel's, and insulted me – he struck me, and I slapped his face, because he used improper language to me; that was the subject I went there about – I was never in custody; one of our presses makes a great noise when it is at work.

COURT. Q. You speak of the office and counting-house – they are parted off by a board? A. Yes, as high as my shoulder – a piece is cut out, so that you can see who comes into the office; the defendant and Peel were in the counting-house, and I even with them, but not in the counting-house – it is too small to hold three; I cannot say whether Barber was in the counting-house any part of the time.

RICHARD POPLE . I am an officer of Union-hall. In May last, Peel was in my custody, with liberty to go out with me to look for a person supposed to have uttered a forged instrument – Mrs. Peel also accompanied me at times; Peel had described the person to me – I was on London-bridge with Mrs. Peel, when the defendant came in sight; Mrs. Peel was standing some distance from me; she ran to me, and said, "There, I think, is the man; there he goes;" I accompanied her, and followed him to about the centre of the bridge, about a hundred yards, and then she spoke to him – I did not hear what she said; he had a handkerchief holding up to his mouth, and when she spoke to him he kept it a little way off, but still kept it before his face; after she had done talking to him I followed him with her – she requested me not to lose sight of him; he went up Fish-street-hill, through White Hart-court, and several other little courts, in and out, till he came to the Cross Keys coach-yard, and into Gracechurch-street; I had him in sight the whole time – he did not call at any place, but kept looking back; he went quite out of the way – it was a bye way to get round; he looked back several times, and I suspected he saw Mrs. Peel – after he got across Cornhill into Bishopsgate-street he got a little way down, then crossed over the way – Mrs. Peel passed me, and got into a gateway; I saw the defendant go into a hosier's or draper's shop, and come out again at the same door in an instant – I saw no more of Mrs. Peel; I followed the prisoner into the Stock Exchange – the turnings he took were quite out of his way; having nobody to assist me, I went for Peel, brought him over with me, went into a court at the back of the Stock Exchange, and there Peel identified the defendant as the man – he was in the court among other persons, not alone; he said he was the man the moment that he saw him, without any doubt whatever- I took him into custody, and told him I wanted him for forgery – he said he did not understand or know anything about it; I got into a coach with Peel, him, and two gentlemen.

Cross-examined. Q. How long had Peel been in your custody? A. Four or five days.

MR. ADOLPHUS. Q. Had he been employed in that time looking for the defendant? A. Day and night.

RICHARD GRAYDEN. I am a brick-maker, and live at Lambeth. The witness Peel is my brother-in-law; I would not believe him on his oath.

MR. ADOLPHUS. Q. Did he marry your sister, or you his? A. I married his – I do not live with her; I allow her a maintenance; I married her in 1818 – I live with no woman now; a woman lives with me.

Richard Grayden 1797-1874. Married to Mary Ann Peel

COURT. Q. How long have you been on bad terms? A. I have not spoken to him for nearly two years; I do not know where my wife lives – I pay the parish 3s. 6d. a week for her, and I have my six children at home to maintain; I think I heard Peel examined in a Court of Justice on the 30th of June, 1830 – I did not contradict what he swore.

ISAAC LATIMER . I was apprenticed to Peel – I would not believe him on his oath.

MR. ADOLPHUS. Q. Have you heard him examined in Courts of Justice? A. I have once, at Union-hball, about obscene prints; and once at the Court of Requests, where he recovered a debt.

HENRY SEWELL. I was apprenticed to Peel – I would not believe him on his oath.

MR. ADOLPHUS. Q. Did you serve out your time with him? A. I left him by the Magistrate's order; my indentures were not cancelled – I heard him examined on his oath about an assault, which he charged me with committing on his wife; I was fined 10s.

JURY to J. W. PEEL. Q. Did you engrave the plate? A. No, Mr. Club; the name of Ellis was put on it according to the copy; I took the order, and gave it to Club to engrave…"

WILLIAM HAYLEY. Deception: fraud.

30th June 1831

Verdict Guilty Sentence Transportation

GUILTY . – Transported for Seven Years

Later there was a Plea for Clemency in 1834, by William Hayley from New South Wales. Dated 28th December 1836 in which he states that John Websdaile Peel is implicated for forging Ellis' name (the printer of the genuine shares). The prisoner's family joined him in New South Wales sailing on the Medway, arriving July 1832. The prisoner sailed on the Portland, arriving March 1832.

The Old Bailey Criminal Court

On the 27th November 1837 at the Old Bailey Criminal Court, JOHN WEBSDALE PEEL, appeared as a witness in the trial of JOHN GODWIN, charged with Theft – stealing from master,

JOHN GODWIN was indicted for stealing, on the 20th of November, 14lbs. weight of lead and antimony mixed together, 'value 1s. 6d., goods of John Peel, his master.

JOHN PEEL . I live in the New Cut, Lambeth, and am a printer. The prisoner was in my service—I lost about 14£lbs. of metal used for types—it consists of lead and antimony—it had been kept in the front kitchen, and is worth about 1s. 6d.

JAMES COULSON . I live at No. 85, Great Saffron-hill, and am a general dealer. About nine o'clock in the evening of the 20th of November I was in the parlour of my house, and the prisoner brought this piece of metal—he said he brought it for sale, and placed it on the counter of the shop for X—he asked no price—I told him I did not think he had come by it honestly—I knew that persons who are possessed of metal of this kind never sell it in that kind of way—he said it was perfectly right—I said "You must give me your name and address, and I must go with you"—I went, and then I found he did live there—I brought him back to my, and told him I should not buy it then, he must call the next morning—directly he was gone I took the metal to the station-house, and asked the inspector for an officer to go and take him.

JAMES MITCHELL (police-constable G 145.) I took the prisoner, and have the metal.

(Property produced, and sworn to.)

Prisoner. I found it in the Blackfriars-road, as I was coming home that night—I wish to know how he can swear to the lead.

JOHN PEEL. I have eight pieces, cast by an apprentice of mine of the name of George Stapleton—on the day the policeman came to me, he asked if I had missed anything—I said I had missed several things—I have lost about 100l. lately—I looked at this, and sent for the ingot that this was cast in, and there were only seven to be found; and only two days before, I saw the prisoner with the bowl we cast the metal in, and I said, "Let it alone"—Stapleton not having strength to take the bowl up at once, he took the metal up by ladlesful, and here is the mark of the small quantities he took up—I did not swear to it the two first times, as knowing his father, I did not wish to do it till I was urged—here is the ingot and the other pieces to match—if there was the slightest doubt, I would not swear to it.

GEORGE STAPLETON . I made some castings for my master, and used a small ladle to pour the metal in with—this piece was one—it fits the ingot exactly, and here are the marks round it—I have no doubt but this is one of those castings.

Verdict: Guilty . Aged 20.— Confined Three Months.

In another case heard at The Old Bailey on 7th April 1845, JOHN PEEL was the victim. In the trial of DAVID MCKIBBIN, for Theft – embezzlement. DAVID MCKIBBIN was indicted for embezzling 2l. 9s. 6d., the monies of John Peel, his master; to which he pleaded GUILTY . Aged 25.— Confined Four Months.

Verdict Guilty – pleaded guilty.

Sentence Imprisonment

On the 14th June 1847, Mr. Peel was at the Old Bailey again this time as a witness name in the trial of WILLIAM GEORGE LIPSCOMB for theft and embezzlement.

JOHN PEEL . I live in the New-cut, Lambeth, and am a printer. The prisoner was in my service as lately as the 20th of April—a person named Snelling was indebted to me for some work done—it was the prisoner's duty to receive money on my account—the course of business was for the money to be entered in the cash-book by the person who received it, the day of the month, and what sort of money was received, and to put the money through a crevice into the desk—I asked the prisoner if Mr. Smith had paid him 9s.—he said I should find it in the book—I have examined the book, and I do not find it entered—the prisoner has not accounted to me for a sum paid by Mr. Snelling.

Prisoner. The money has been paid to me, and not entered in the cash-book; he asked me if I had received Mr. Smith's; I told him I had; I received the three sums, the 9s. 6d., 9s., and 1l. 2s. 6d., but unfortunately did not enter them in the cash-book.

JOHN PEEL re-examined. Q. How many day's delay was there in the entry in the cash-book? A. I had not questioned him about Mr. Snelling's money—I only asked him about Mr. Smith's—I discharged him for intoxication—I wondered how he got the money.

RICHARD SNELLING, Jun. I am clerk to Messrs. Shield and Co. I knew the prisoner in the prosecutor's service—on the 3rd of April he brought this bill of 1l. 2s. 6d.—I paid him, and he receipted the bill.

CHARLES SMITH. I knew the prisoner as servant to the prosecutor—he brought me a bill of 9s. on the 15th of April—he told me Mr. Peel was very poorly—I told him to receipt the bill—I gave him the money.

NATHANIEL FREDERICK OKEY. I keep the Hero of Waterloo, in Waterloo-road. The prisoner produced this bill for 9s. 6d. to me on the 19th of April—I paid him the amount—he receipted the bill.

HENRY CHAMPION (police-constable F 107.) I apprehended the prisoner.

JOHN PEEL re-examined. Q. Did the prisoner ever either of these bills in the cash-book? A. He did not—he he did not communicate to me of his own accord that he had received them—he did not admit that he had received any of them, and omitted to enter it—I spoke to him about Mr. Smith's—he said he had entered that—the others I have found out since—he made no communication to me about them—I discharged him about the 20th of April—he did not leave my place till the 24th.

Prisoner. It might have passed my memory; I have been in the habit of receiving money, and always entered it in the cash-book: I have omitted to enter this, but if I had been disposed to have made off with money, I might have made off with more than this; I had a great deal of money; I have delivered this money faithfully up to Mr. Peel. Witness. His duty was to put in into the desk, not to give it to me, but put it down in the book—I compared the money with the book day by day—I did not find there was too much—it always tallied with the book—two or three persons take money—they have order to put down what money they receive, and the description of it—I found no such sums as these in the desk—I found no paper that disclosed he had received this money, not any money unaccounted for—I am able to swear that the 1l. 2s. 6d. was not paid to me in the shop.

Verdict Guilty.

Sentence Imprisonment.

GUILTY.— Confined Six Months.

Perhaps the most famous trial Mr. Peel took part in concerned Charles-Louis Napoleon Bonaparte, later known as Louis Napoleon and then Napoleon III.

Charles Louis Napoleon, 1849

On 25 May 1846, with the assistance of his doctor and other friends on the outside, Charles-Louis Napoleon disguised himself as a laborer carrying lumber, and walked out of the prison he had been held at in France. A carriage was waiting to take him to the coast and then by boat to England. A month after his escape, his father Louis died, making Louis Napoleon the clear heir to the Bonaparte dynasty.

Another period of exile in London followed. He quickly resumed his place in British society. He lived on King Street in St James's, London, went to the theatre and hunted, renewed his acquaintance with Benjamin Disraeli, and met Charles Dickens. He went back to his studies at the British Museum. He had an affair with the actress Rachel, the most famous French actress of the period, during her tours to Britain. More important for his future career, he had an affair with the wealthy heiress Harriet Howard (1823–1865). They met in 1846, soon after his return to Britain. They began to live together, she took in his two illegitimate children and raised them with her own son, and she provided financing for his political plans so that, when the moment came, he could return to France. It was while trying to fund this return to France that Charles-Louis Napoleon became involved with Charles Pollard.

JOHN WEBSDALE PEEL sat on the Jury. Recorded in the archives of The Old Bailey as the Front matter from Proceedings, 5th July 1847. CHARLES POLLARD ,- Theft, simple larceny. 5th July 1847. CHARLES POLLARD was indicted for stealing, on the 15th of June, 2 bills of exchange for the payment and value of 1000l. each, property of Charles Louis Napoleon Bonaparte, a Prince of Kingdom of France.

LIST OF JURORS.

First Jury: - Joseph Hart, William Scriven, Thomas Augustus Ring, William Deller,

Edward Green, John Websdale Peel, Alfred Pocock, Charles Henry Laws, John Taylor,

James Barber, Samuel Pearce, James Meadows

CENTRAL CRIMINAL COURT.

CARROLL, MAYOR. NINTH SESSION.

CHARLES POLLARD was indicted for stealing, on the 15th of June, 2 bills of exchange for the payment and value of 1000l. each property of Charles Louis Napoleon Bonaparte, a Prince of Kingdom of France:

MESSRS. CLARKSON and BODKIN conducted Prosecution.

THE PRINCE CHARLES LOUIS NAPOLEON BONAPARTE. My name is Charles Louis Napoleon Bonaparte—I am a son of the late King of Holland—I reside at No. 3, King-street, St. James's. In the month of June last, in consequence of the non-arrival of a remittance from Florence, I was desirous of obtaining 2000l. for a temporary purpose—I communicated that wish to Mr. Orsi, who is acting as my secretary—on the 10th of June I received this letter by the post—(looking at it)—I saw the prisoner the day afterwards, and he told me he was the man that wrote to me the day before—(read—"Private—Cornhill, June 10th, 1847—Mr. Pollard presents respect to Prince Napolean, and Mr. P. will do himself the honour of calling upon the Prince to-morrow morning at twelve o'clock on private business. Prince Napolean.") On the following day he came to my house in King-street, and introduced himself as the writer of that letter—he was at that time a perfect stranger to me—he told me that he had heard I wished to have some money; and that he had 2000l., 3000l., or 4000l. to offer if I wished it—I told him I was not quite sure that I should want it; that I was about selling out several shares in railways, which I had at that moment—I asked him how he knew I wanted money—his answer was that he was a man of business; that it was his business to procure money for noblemen; and if such was the case that they always came to him—I asked him about the terms, and he was to take five per cent.—I asked his address—he told me he was living at No. 10, Essex-street, Strand—I then told him to come back on the following Monday, that would be the 14th...

The COURT was of opinion that the prisoner's presenting the stamps to the Prince, upon which he drew the bill, gave the Prince a property in them; but that he parted with that property in order to obtain the money; (distinguishing the present case from that of a servant or agent intrusted with notes or bills for a specific purpose, such as to change or discount,) and that the fraudulent intention of the prisoner could not affect that question.

The prisoner was accordingly
ACQUITTED.

Before Mr. Justice Maule.

Chapter Six – Nero's Rescue

> MIRACULOUS PRESERVATION of the LIVES of TWO CHILDREN by a NEWFOUNDLAND DOG.
>
> On Saturday afternoon, between three and four o'clock, two little boys, one six years of age, the other about nine, sons of Mr. HORNCROFT, of No. 6, Bridge-row, Pimlico, were playing on the banks of the Grosvenor Canal at Pimlico, and climbing up one of the cranes used for unloading the barges, when the youngest accidentally fell off the head of the crane into the water, a height of about ten feet. The eldest immediately jumped into the Canal after him, when after a short struggle they both went down. At this moment Mr. PEEL, the printer, in the New Cut, Lambeth, accompanied by Mr. REGAN, comedian of Astley's, chanced to pass with his celebrated Newfoundland dog Nero, well known for his performances in various pieces at the different Theatres. Mr. PEEL, who saw the children sink, instantly threw a pebble to the spot, and Nero plunged in, dived at the place, and almost instantly brought up the eldest boy. As he was swimming with him to the shore the clothes tore that the dog had holding, and the boy sunk again, but was quickly recovered by the dog, and brought safe on shore. The youngest had appeared twice during the time, and no sooner had Nero placed the boy in safety than he plunged in a second time; and, after diving for a few seconds, he appeared with the youngest boy, and brought him on shore in a state of complete exhaustion. By this time upwards of two hundred people had assembled, and the children were conveyed to the nearest public-house, where they soon recovered. Every person appeared anxious to see the dog that had saved the children's lives, and the caresses he received from the crowd were overwhelming.

The Morning Post 11th March 1834

On Saturday 8th March 1834 Mr. Peel was walking with his friend Mr. Regan and his Newfoundland dog, Nero – from Astley's, beside the Grosvenor Canal, Pimlico. When he saw two boys, one aged six, the other nine, get into difficulties in the canal. What happened next was fully reported in the Newspapers of the time.

MIRACULOUS PRESERVATION of the LIVES of TWO CHILDREN by a NEWFOUNDLAND DOG.

On Saturday afternoon, between three and four o'clock, two little boys, one six years of age, the other about nine, sons of Mr. Horncroft, of No. 6, Bridge-row, Pimlico, were playing on the banks of the Grosvenor Canal at Pimlico, and climbing up one of the cranes used for unloading the barges, when the youngest accidentally fell off the head of the crane into the water, a height of about ten feet. The eldest immediately jumped into the Canal after him, when after a short struggle, they both went down. At this moment Mr. Peel, the printer, in the New Cut, Lambeth, accompanied by Mr. Regan, comedian of Astley's, chanced to pass with his celebrated Newfoundland dog Nero, well known for his performances in various pieces at the different Theatres. Mr. Peel, who saw the children sink, instantly threw a pebble to the spot, and Nero plunged in, dived at the place, and almost instantly brought up the eldest boy. As he was swimming with him to the shore the clothes tore that the dog had holding, and the boy sunk again, but was quickly recovered by the dog, and brought safe on shore. The youngest had appeared twice during the time, and no sooner had Nero placed the boy in safety than he plunged in a second time; after diving for a few seconds, he appeared with the youngest boy, and brought him on shore in a state of complete exhaustion. By this time upwards of two hundred people had assembled, and the children were conveyed to the nearest public-house, where they soon recovered. Every person appeared anxious to see the dog that had saved the children's lives, and the caresses he received from the crowd were overwhelming.

Brought Safe on Shore - A Newfoundland Dog makes a Rescue.

Mr. Horncroft, the father of the children, on being informed of circumstance, expressed his acknowledgments to Mr. Peel, and gave a grand dinner, at which Nero appeared as the principal guest, and harmlessly played with the children whom he had saved from a watery grave.

Chapter Seven – The Newspapers

Newspapers not only reported on Mr. Peel's exploits at the Courts of Justice, or beside the Grosvenor-canal in Pimlico. They also provided a means of advertising forthcoming events. Mr. Peel used newspaper classified advertisements to sell items, and to advertise his Printing-Office's products and services. In short, they were used to generally promote Mr. Peel's business, and himself.

Newspaper classified advertising was typically short, as they were charged for by the line or word. Usually they did not allow images, and were one newspaper column wide. The Morning Advertiser, dated Thursday 20 October 1842, for example, ran the following classified advertisement:

Forget It Not: Wooden Letter-Presses and Copper-Plate. Ditto given away almost. Inquire at Peel's Printing-office, 74, New Cut nearly opposite The Victoria Theatre.

While Reynold's Newspaper on Sunday 20 August 1848 advertised a promotional meal with moderate charges for John Websdale Peel's friends and the public, at THE ROYAL VICTORIA TAVERN – FORGET IT NOT, given by MR. PEEL, Printer, of The New-cut… next door to The Victoria Theatre…

The British Museum is home to a newspaper cutting (object number – 1980,U.1107). It is an article entitled 'Sam Scott, the Diver', dating from January 1841 showing Samuel G Scott diving from a scaffold on Southwark Bridge into the Thames. Pasted onto a backing sheet of the same sheet is an advertisement for Scott's dives for the week of 21 December 1840, with a woodcut of a hand with finger pointing at the word 'Notice!!' 1840-1841. Wood-engraving and letterpress;

Printed by: J W Peel (letterpress printer of advertisement)

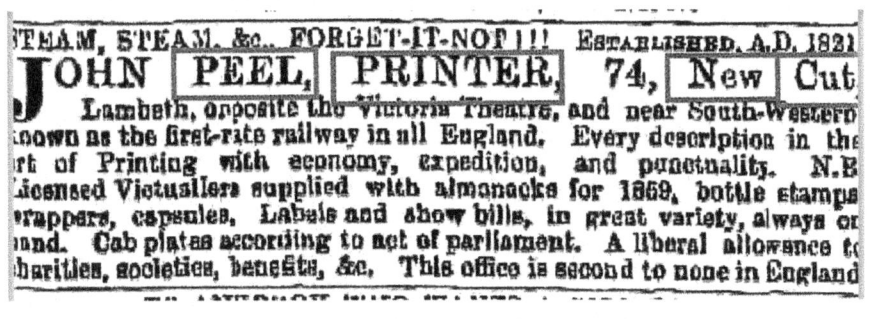

The Era, December 1858

The Era, ran an advertisement on Sunday 5 December, and Sunday 19 December 1858 describing the range of products supplied by Mr. Peel's Printing Press.

STEAM, STEAM, &c, FORGET-IT-NOT!!! Established, A.D. 1821.

JOHN PEEL, PRINTER, 74, New Cut, Lambeth, opposite the Victoria Theatre, and near South-Western, known as the first-rate railway in all England. Every description in the art of Printing with economy, expedition, and punctuality. N.B. Licensed Victuallers supplied with almanacks for 1859, bottle stamps, wrappers, capsules, labels and show bills, in great variety, always on hand. Cab plates according to act of parliament. A liberal allowance to charities, societies, benefits, &c. This office is second to none in England.

The Morning Post Tuesday 3 August 1841 reported that on April 29th 1831, Mr. Peel issued an advertisement in the form of a Bank of England £5 Note. The note stated: Bank of Engraving- I promise to execute letter-press or copper plate cards in the first style of elegance, as also bills, circulars, &c, with the greatest despatch, or forfeit Five Pounds - For Self and Co., "J, W. Peel, 9 Charlotte-terrace, New Cut, Lambeth. 1831. April 29th."

At Marylebone Magistrates Court on Monday 2nd August 1841: "A well-dressed young man, named William Reader was brought up in custody, charged with having fraudulently obtained five sovereigns." He had asked for change for a £5 Note from Mr. Thomas Marchant, a butcher. Examining the note properly, Mr. Marchant proved it to be Mr. Peel's £5 advertisement.

Chapter Eight – Mr. Peel's Printing Office

Mr. Peel's printing office on New Cut, Lambeth, relied on a team of men and women working well together. At any given moment in time this team consisted of Apprentices, Journeymen, Compositors and type makers, workers of the Steam-Machine Press, stackers and sorters. Mr. Peel even employed a traveller given the task of finding new work and promoting the business. Sophia Peel, his wife, and later Cecilia Stapleton, his partner, and then Cecilia Sheen, Mr. Peel's daughter, contributed greatly to the success of the business.

Many Individuals were employed at Mr. Peel's Printing Establishment on New Cut over the years 1823-1859 including:

JOHN (STAPLETON) PEEL – the son of John Websdale Peel. He was brought up in the business. At the time of the 1851 Census, he was only 16, his profession is described as a Printer. In 1860, his actions are recorded in the newspapers. Impatient with the executors of his father's will he behaves impetuously...John Peel called on Mr. Johnson, a leasee of the City of London Theatre and one of the executors... he knocked violently at the door, so as to alarm the inmates and caused the neighbours to rush to their door. He also called out the name of Mr. Johnson in a loud voice, and asked him why he did not pay him the money left to him by his father? It was while the servant, Mrs. Johnson and a female relative were trying to remove John Peel that Mr.Johnson stepped forward and struck him a severe blow. For which Mr. Johnson was fined 10 shillings, with costs.

By 1861, John Peel had married Elizabeth and had two children, Henry and Joseph Thomas, and his printing business had moved to 11 William Street, Lambeth.

CECELIA STAPLETON PEEL (SHEEN) – John Websdale Peel's daughter. She would have fulfilled a vital role in the running of the business. With her brother, John, she had been brought-up in New Cut, Lambeth. On Wednesday 28th 1860, she gave evidence to The Court of Common Pleas during the legal proceedings taken by Mrs. McNabb. As Cecelia Sheen, she states that she was a servant to Mr.Peel, and that she left to get married. From June 1858 – May 1859 ... "Mr.Peel was very well then, but he was given to drink."

GEORGE STAPLETON – was born on January 19th 1821. His father James Stapleton , was a cook. His mother became Mr. Peel's partner c.1834; living and working in New Cut. When he was about 15, he became an apprentice to Mr. Peel.

On the 27th November 1837 George Stapleton gave evidence in the trial of another of John Websdale Peel's apprentices, John Godwin. Godwin was accused of stealing lead and antimony used in the making of type. Mr. Peel says:" I have eight pieces, cast by an apprentice of mine of the name of George Stapleton – on the day the policeman came to me, he asked if I had missed anything – I said I had missed several things ..... only two days before, I saw the prisoner with the bowl we cast metal in, and I said "Let it alone" – Stapleton not having the strength to take the bowl up at once, he took the metal up by ladlesfull, and here is the mark of the small quantities he took up...

Stapleton when cross-examined stated : I made some castings for my master, and used a small ladle to pour the metal in with – this piece was one – it fits the ingot exactly, and here are the marks around it – I have no doubt but this is one of those castings.

Godwin was found guilty and confined for three months.

The 1841 Census for New Cut, Lambeth, shows George Stapleton an apprentice, aged 20, living with the Peel family. On 3rd March 1844, banns are read out at St.Mary's Church, Lambeth signalling George's forth-coming marriage. However, he has to wait until December 26th 1844 before he can marry Isabella Sarah Hawkins at St. John the Evangelist, Lambeth. Isabella's father, John Gilbert Hayne Hawkins is described in the record as a Lieutenant in the Royal Marines.

George Stapleton became a Master Printer in his own right. The Census for 1851 and 1861, and The Post Office Directories for 1850, and 1860, all indicating that he worked and lived at 94 Waterloo Road. Here he continued a long association with the theatre and circus by producing numerous posters and handbills for such venues as The Royal Surrey Zoological Gardens, and The Royal Vauxhall Gardens.

In early 1870 George Stapleton's death, at the age of 49, was unexpected. Yet within the year his widow, Isabella Sarah Stapleton had remarried.

HENRY JOHN MARR – Compositor – Gave evidence at the Court of Common Pleas regarding Probate of Mr. Peel's will. – As reported in Reynold's Newspaper, Monday 3rd December 1860. Marr said... "he was in the employ of Mr. Peel in 1856, and had been in his service altogether sixteen years. Mr. Peel had a wife, but she was not living with him nor was there during part of 1856 a soul in the house with him. He talked in the latter part of November about engaging a housekeeper. Mr.Peel asked the witness to accompany him to the Circassian Stores. On the way witness asked him who he thought of having for a housekeeper, and Mr. Peel said "Mrs.McNabb." In witness presence Mr. Peel offered her 18 pounds a year wages, and two months afterwards she came with her boxes to Mr. Peel's, and Mr. Peel said he had engaged with her at 18 pounds a year, and that witness and the others in the house were to consider her as housekeeper. Mr. Serjeant Ballantine said, "He would not contradict the evidence which had been given by Mr. Marr, who seemed a very respectable man..."

A year after visiting the Circassian Stores with Mr. Peel, Henry John Marr married Charlotte Emery, at St. Mary's Parish Church, Newington. The 1861 Census records the Marrs living at 7 York Road, Waterloo Road, Lambeth with their daughter Alice Mary, and Charlotte's mother Mary Emery. In 1868 Henry John Marr dies, at the early age of 43. Three years later and the Census of 1871 shows Charlotte Marr living at 35 Richmond Street, Lambeth, together with Alice Mary aged 10, Charlotte aged 6, and Elizabeth aged 3.

ISAAC LATIMER – Apprentice – On the 31st June Isaac Latimer stands up at The Old Bailey in the case against William Hayley, and declares, " I was apprenticed to Mr. Peel – I would not believe him on his oath."

Isaac Latimer, later became editor of the Plymouth and Devonport Weekly Journal. He met and married his wife Mary, formerly Paddon, whilst working on the West Briton in Truro. They had six children. Selina Frances was the third child and the only girl. She spoke in later life of the fact that her father gave all his family of six 'a good education and start of life.'

In 1860 Isaac Latimer launched a new daily paper, Western Daily Mercury, from offices in Frankfort Street. This paper reflected his Liberalism and his radical values of religious toleration and civil liberty. Latimer was a member (and sometime chairman) of the Plymouth Liberal Association; became a town councillor and Mayor; a member of the Deputy Chamber of Commerce; of the Western Temperance League; and a town council member of the Plymouth Board of Guardians.

Mary Latimer died in 1879, but her daughter Frances and Isaac were to remain companions and allies until his death twenty years later. Isaac enjoyed travelling and writing about his experiences, and Frances always accompanied him. Together they embarked on ambitious projects such as the formation of a Women's Liberal Association, and the enfranchisement of women. Isaac Latimer died in September 1898.

This information from The Devonshire History Society.

CHARLES FREDERICK BARBER – Journeyman – Had lived with Mr. Peel since March 1830, before giving his evidence at The Old Bailey, on the 30th June 1831. As a journeyman, Charles would have had a higher status than the apprentices. Having successfully completed an official apprenticeship himself. In fact, Mr. Peel states that Barber "superintends my business when I am out…"

Charles Barber's evidence during the trial of William Hayley provides a good description of how the premises in New Cut is laid out. He also describes the working of the press and the distribution of the employees within the business. Giving a brief – behind the scenes insight into the day to day running of a 19th century London printers office.

There were other individuals recorded as working at Mr. Peel's Printing Office New Cut:

Thomas Moss – Apprentice – (1841 Census), Henry Sewell – Apprentice – (1831 Old Bailey),

John Godwin – Apprentice – (1837 Old Bailey), David McKibben – Apprentice – (1845 Old Bailey), William George Lipscomb – Apprentice – (1847 Old Bailey), and Charles W. Herbert – Traveller – 1856 – (Court of Common Pleas 1860)

Chapter Nine – The Steam Machine

In his testimony at the Old Bailey 30 June 1831 John Websdale Peel gives a description of the printing office at 9 New Cut "…the office is divided – there are two rooms, the press and composing rooms…" Mrs. Peel adds "… One of our presses makes a great noise when it is at work…" When questioned about the office and a counting house being parted by a board, she explains "… Yes, as high as my shoulder – a piece is cut-out, so that you can see who comes into the office…"

Charles Frederick Barber – Journeyman to John Websdale Peel states "… the office where we work has a deal of bustle in it there were two more men at work in the office, about four yards from the master, but you cannot hear while the press is going…"

The Times set up the first steam-powered printing machine in Fleet Street. On 29 November 1814, a new steam-powered double-cylinder printing press from Friedrich Koenig and Andreas Bauer was used to print The Times in London.

No record exists of the type of steam-powered printing press used by Mr. Peel. There was, however, a nearby factory that Mr. Peel would have been aware of. The works of Robert Hoe & Co. Ltd, makers of printing presses and other printing equipment. Their main factory, situated on the south side of Borough Road, included No. 109-112, a former chapel and several premises in the appropriately named Rotary Street.

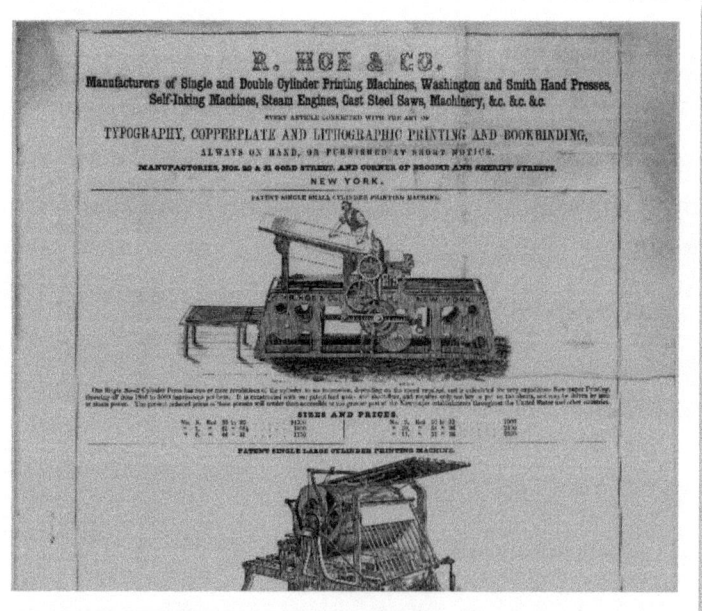

R. Hoe's Catalogue with Steam Machine Press 1846

Needing labour to operate it, and coal to drive it. Mr. Peel's steam press would have provided increased speed, and reliability. This creative use of new steam technologies, careful attention to the firm's reputation, and excellent business choices brought commercial success to Mr. Peel's Printing Office.

Commercial success mirrored by the numerous entries in the Business and Trade directories of the time. Throughout his working life J. W. Peel, Printer, New Cut. appeared in the Trade directories. These were produced to help promote and facilitate trade and commerce. A directory would include a general description of the town or area as well as details on local transportation, churches, schools, government offices and officials, shops, and businesses. Sometimes more detailed information on specific people, such as businessmen, traders, shopkeepers, was included as well.

Businesses such as Foster and Winstone, manufacturers of printing ink, were included in the Trade Directories. Mr. Peel obtained his printing ink from Foster and Winstone. There are records of a legal case brought in 1860, against the Executors of Mr. Peel's estate, by Benjamin Winstone of Foster and ,Winstone, manufacturers of printing ink, 100-101 Shoe Lane, London. It was Benjamin Winstone who supplied the Bank of England with note printing-ink as his great chemical knowledge allowed the production of ink of the highest order.

But the printing trade was not always plain sailing. At The Old Bailey on 27 November 1837 John Godwin, in service to John Websdale Peel, was indicted for stealing 14lbs.weight of lead and antimony mixed together, value one shilling and six pence. As John W. Peel says. "I lost about 14 lbs. of metal used for types - it consists of lead and antimony- it had been kept in the front kitchen, and is worth about 1s. 6d." "...I saw the prisoner with the bowl we cast the metal in..."

Type Metal was an alloy of lead, antimony and tin. Lead soft and easily cast was given the hardness it needs to endure the printing process by adding antimony and tin. Also giving a sharper casting from the mould to produce clear, easily read, printed text. There were, however, consequences.

Lead is highly toxic and poisonous at low concentrations. It can cause an increase in violent behaviour, brain damage, intellectual disability, abdominal pain, constipation, headaches, irritability, memory problems, tingling in the hands and feet. Constant exposure to Antimony can result in effects similar to arsenic poisoning and may cause respiratory irritation, pneumoconiosis, antimony spots on the skin, gastrointestinal symptoms, and cardiac problems. In addition, antimony trioxide is potentially carcinogenic.

Chapter Ten – Death

According to Cecilia, his daughter: "The day Mr. Peel died Mrs. McNabb lay on the hearth-rug in front of the fire quite drunk, and Mr. Edmonds, the doctor, had to step over her to get to Mr. Peel."

In Reynold's Newspaper , Sunday 2nd December 1860, Charles W. Herbert employed by Mr. Peel as a traveller, recounts: " Mr. Peel died on the 6th of December, 1859, and the plaintiff got drunk the night that he died. They had in a pint of gin, but she said that the cat had knocked it over. She lay down drank on the mattress, and afterwards she got up and said, "Where is little Jemmy" (Mr. Peel)? Witness said, "Don't make a noise; he has been gone (dead) this twenty minutes." She asked for some gin, but witness said it was all gone."

A southerly storm gave way to hail as John Websdale Peel, Master Printer, died at 74, New Cut, Lambeth, London. His Death Certificate records the date 6th December 1859.

The Cause of Death, noted as Jaundice with disease of Liver and Kidneys. Certified.

Record of Mr. Peel's Burial. Norwood Cemetry, Lambeth

Mr. Peel was buried in Norwood Cemetery on the 12th December 1859.

It was the start of a particularly cold spell. For the next three days London was frozen.

A week later, and heavy snow blanketed Mr. Peel's grave.

૰૰૰

Chapter Eleven – The Probate Case

Executors of Mr. Peel's will were announced in the Times and The Morning Advertiser. They were Mr. John Johnson of Number Nine, Albert Street, Newington, and Edmund Edmunds of 52 New Cut, Lambeth.

A few months later, impatient with the executors of his father's will, John Stapleton Peel behaves impetuously... John Peel called on Mr. Johnson, a leasee of the City of London Theatre and one of the executors.... he knocked violently at the door, so as to alarm the inmates and caused the neighbours to rush to their door. He also called out the name of Mr. Johnson in a loud voice, and asked him why he did not pay him the money left to him by his father. It was while the servant, Mrs. Johnson and a female relative were trying to remove John Peel that Mr. Johnson stepped forward and struck him a severe blow. For which Mr. Johnson was fined 10 shillings, with costs.

John Peel had to wait over a year for a resolution to the situation, because there followed a court case challenging the executors of Mr. Peel's will.

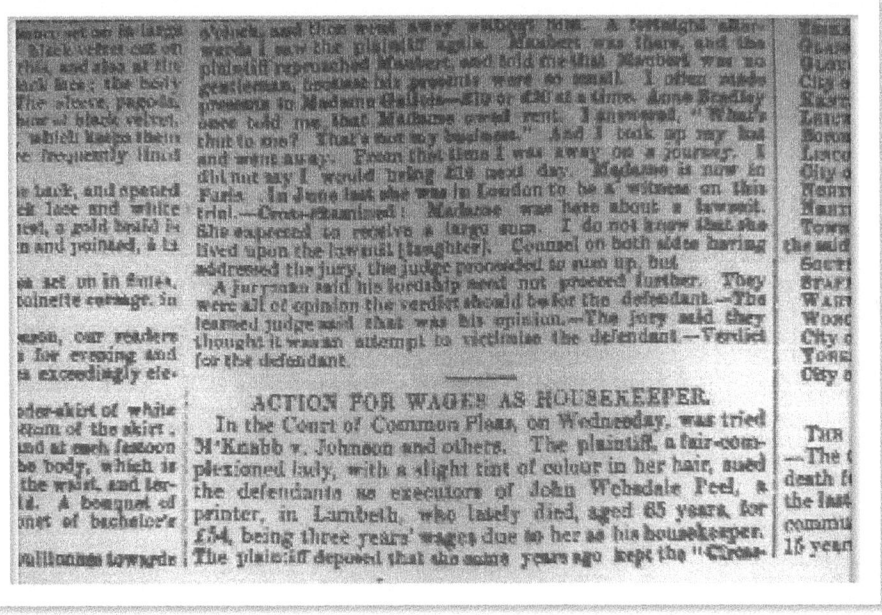

Picture Twenty Four – The Court Case Reported. December 1860

A number of newspapers reported on the court case contesting the will: McNabb v Johnson and Others, in the Court of Common Pleas. These included; Lloyd's Weekly Newspaper. Sunday 2 December 1860, Reynolds Newspaper, Sunday 2 December 1860, The Era, Sunday 2 December 1860, The Morning Post, Thursday 29 November 1859, and The Observer 3 December 1860.

The Enniskillen Chronicle and Erne Packet,. Thursday 6th December 1860 published their version of the story of Mrs. McNabb's claim on Mr. Peel's will:

'THE FAIR (BUT VERY WET) CIRCASSIAN.'

COURT OF COMMON PLEAS, London, November 28 .1860

McNabb v. Johnson and Others.—The plaintiff in this case was a very fair complexioned lady, with the slightiest possible hint of colour in her hair, and she sued the executors of John Websdale Peel, a printer of Lambeth, as died a short time ago, aged sixty five years, to recover £54 for three years wages due her as his "housekeeper."

Mr. Sergeant' Tozer and Mr. Pritchard appeared for the plaintiff; and Mr. Sergeant Ballantine and Mr Prentice for the defendants.

The plaintiff was called to give evidence, and she stated that three or four years ago she kept the Circassian Stores, in Drury lane, an establishment which was formerly known as the Harlequin. Mr. Peel used to come to her house, and she told him that the business did not answer, she must give it up. Mr. Peel asked her to become his housekeeper, offering her £18 a year wages. She afterwards agreed to become his housekeeper and when she disposed of her property at the Circassian Stores, she went to Mr. Peel's. She remained in the position of his housekeeper for three years, but did not receive any wages during that time. She had some money of her own. Therefore could buy necessaries, without receiving her wages.

'Cross examined by Mr. Sergeant Ballantine Mr. Peel printed bills for her whilst at the Circassian Stores, and that was how she became acquainted with him. She did not know that those bills stated that a fair Circassian lady, and daughter of that distinguished chieftain Schamy, was to be seen at the bar. (Laughter.) Witness was no scholar, and could not read the bill. The only bills she had printed were about a lady of colour.

Mr. Sergeant Ballantine; But she was not the fair Circassian.

Witness: No.I was the only fair Cicassian there. (Renewed laughter.) Though Mr. Peel frequented her house, she did not know that he got drunk there. There was not every night a private party. Composed of her the lady of colour and Mr. Peel. (a laugh), it was all public. Whilst acting as Mr. Peel's house-keeper, she did not sleep in his bed, not until he became very ill and feeble that he could not be left at night.

Mr. Sergeant Ballantine; Whilst he was a dreadful invalid, have you had chops, kidneys, and steaks in bed together, for breakfast, and washed them down with gin? (Laughter.)

Witness; He was an invalid, both in his hands and in his feet. They might have had these things.

To the Judge: She had nothing more than nurses ordinarily have. (Renewed laughter)

Examination continued: It was months and months before she went to his bed. She used not to get drunk most days. She was not uselessly drunk the night before his death. When she went to Mr. Peel's she took with her a girl to stay a day or two until she could get her a place. She stayed for a month. She and the girl had a few words, and then the girl left. There was no fight. The girl struck witness, but witness did not strike the girl. There was a servant also who left, but witness had no quarrel or fight with her. Mr Peel left her £50 by will. Her attorney originally demanded four years wages, £5 money lent, and the restoration of two spade guineas, a chain, eye-glass, silk dress, &n; but there was a mistake as to twelve-months' wages. Mr. Peel was an irritable man, but they did not fight; there was nothing more than words.

Charles-W-Herbert had been in the employment of the deceased as a traveller. Witness went to see the plaintiff at Drury lane, because Peel told him that he would show him the fairest flower that ever bloomed, and give him some tripe for supper, (Loud laughter.) In December 1856, witness went to the plaintiff at the request of Mr. Peel. She said she was going to leave because business did not pay. Mr. Dodd, a master farrier used to visit her, and Mr Peel was very jealous of Dodd and said in witness's hearing, Jess, if you would like to come to my house, there is a home for you. She said she would rather not, for she had some friends at Hackney whom she could go to. Mr.Peel said, Charley (witness) will do everything requisite; you come home to me. Witness afterwards saw her into the cab that was to take her to Mr.Peel's house, witness having first taken the message from Mr.Peel – Come home as soon as you can. He gave her the key of the plaintiff's house and said, There is the key; you know how to open the door. You are to go and see Mr.Peel instantly you get there." This was at four o'clock in the morning. On the following day witness went up to Mr.Peel's bedroom according to custom, as Mr.Peel, always wished to see him to have a drop of gin together. (laughter). The servant, however, said, You can't go up yet; they are not up. He said, "Who?" and she replied, "Mistress and your governor." When the plaintiff came down, she said, "You can go up now, Jemmy wants to see you." He had seen the plaintiff and Mr.Peel in bed hundreds of times together. He used to prepare their breakfast. "Sometimes they said they would like ham and eggs, sometimes kidneys, sometimes a rump-steak, and sometimes a mushroom cooked with it. (loud laughter) When he took breakfast up she used say, "Charley, will you have a toothful?" then witness used to have a bit. (Renewed laughter.)

Mr Sergeant Tozer said he would not put any questions relative to this part of the case.

Mr. Sergeant Ballentine : These inquiries are the only means we have of getting at the domestic manners of "the fair Circassian." (Laughter,)

Witness continued. The plaintiff was the habit of getting drunk; they all used to get drunk together (laughter.) She very often got drunk; Mr Peel and she were in the habit ol quarrelling, and witness had got between them, and so had Mr.Peel's daughter. Mr. Peel died on the 5th of December 1859, and the plaintiff got drunk on the night that he died. They had a pint of gin, and she said that the cat had knocked it over; she lay down drunk on the mattress, and afterwards she got up, and said Where is little Jemmy (Mr Peel.)? Witness said "Don't make a noise; he has been gone (dead) this twenty minutes." She asked for some gin, but witness said it was all gone.

There was also some evidence to show that the plaintiff had the management of the deceased's monetary affairs, and frequently received money on his account.

His lordship left it to the jury to say whether there had been any contract to hire the plaintiff as housekeeper; and, if so, whether there had been any payment to her. 'The executors had done no more than their duty—apart from any considerations as to the testator — in requiring an examination in open court, before a jury, into the claim of the plaintiff.

The jury found a verdict for the defendant.

Revised Probate Document. December 1862. Following the Trial.

PART TWO

MR. PEEL'S POSTERS
The Work of John Websdale Peel (1794-1859)

Chapter Twelve – Broadsheets

During the 19th century printing became one of London's major industries. Lambeth and Southwark, in particular became a focal-point for wood-engravers, compositors and printers. All in constant demand.

The abolition of the Theatres Act of 1843, with its regulations hindering Theatre productions, resulted in a rapid growth in the number of theatres in London. They all needed posters and handbills to promote the acts, and to call attention to the venue and event.

Mr. Peel was on hand to supply them. The Posters and handbills formed the vast majority of Mr. Peel's output as a printer. They often included the innovative use of design, images, copy and colour. From archives held in England, and America it is now possible to chart the evolution of Mr. Peel's posters from their beginnings in the 1820's, to the final years of 1850.

The Origin of the Fairlop Oak

One of the earliest surviving examples of Mr. Peel's work is the 1824 Fairlop Oak Broadsheet:

THE ORIGIN OF THE FAIRLOP OAK, &c. Taken from an original drawing by an eminent artist and printed off a wood cut engraved on a block of the celebrated tree.

The Fairlop Oak stood in Hainault Forest when much of the area was covered in trees. The Oak is said to have had a trunk sixty-six feet in circumference. An annual fair was held in the forest, using the oak as a focal point. It took place on the first Friday of July every year. In June 1805, the oak tree caught fire, and in 1820 it was finally blown down.

Mr. Peel obtained some wood from this fallen oak and made a woodcut from it for his broadsheet of 1824. The Broadsheet contains the lyrics of a song from the Block Makers Boat Song, sung by Mr. Hemingway. Mr. Hemingway, a ballad singer arrived at the fair in a boat on wheels which was decked in flags and bunting.

Inscribed Box. From the wood of The Fairlop Oak.

*This picture was taken outside the Kings Arms in Mile End Road.
It is thought that the man in the light coat and hat seated in
the centre of the boat is Mr Hemingway.*

J. W. Peel later had a small box made, which he inscribed in pen; "A gift of J W Peel to Mr. Hemingway 1834. Cut out of the old Oak." It can be seen in the Redbridge Museum, Edmonton, London; donated to the museum by relatives of Mr. Hemingway.

Another Broadsheet headlined DEATH IN A RAGE was published by J. W. Peel in 1832. This was printed in the wake of the cholera epidemic of 1832. The cholera epidemic spread across England, Ireland and Scotland. Numbers infected grew rapidly, and by 1 August 1832 there were 22,960 cases with 8,595 deaths. The mortality rate increased with the heat of the summer. It would not be until the winter, and the end of 1832, that the disease eventually ran its course.

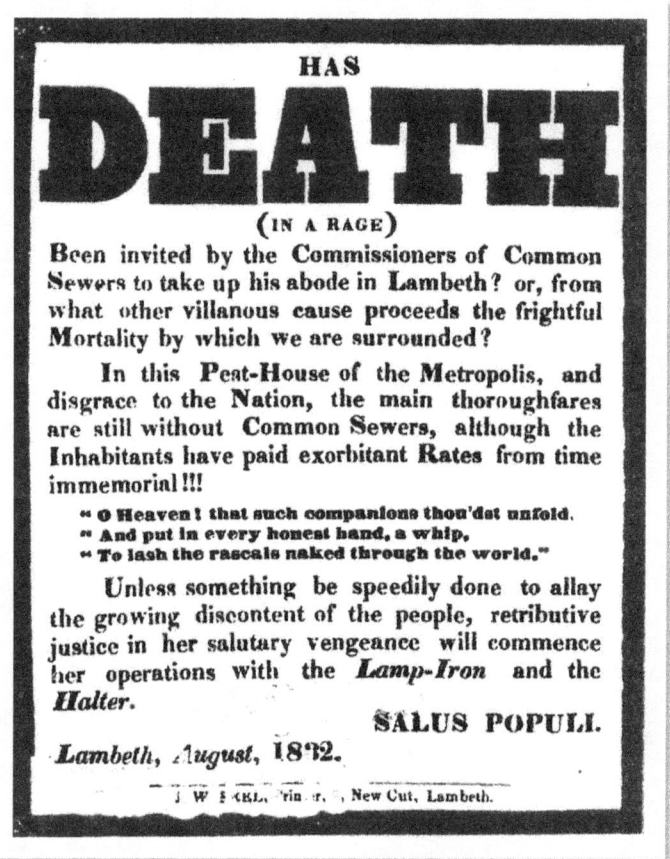

Death in a Rage

Cholera had struck London swiftly. By 21 February 1832, just over a week after the first cases, there were 40 cases in total in Limehouse, Southwark and Lambeth. Among those who lived on the river. The Atlas published an opinion piece saying that since the cholera's first victims were in the east, in the crowded borough of Southwark and in the marshy low grounds of Lambeth. This was an indication that it would be confined to the 'ill-fed and ill-clothed' and that the respectable ranks of life and fashionable society are sure to be spared. It was probably opinions such as these that prompted Mr. Peel's Broadsheet - Death in a Rage. It was death that had shaped John Websdale Peel's life. By the time he was eighteen he had lost nearly all of his closest family. All but his sister Mary.

Has DEATH (In A Rage) been invited by the Commissioners of Common Sewers to take up his abode in Lambeth? Or, from what other villainous cause proceeds the frightful mortality by which we are surrounded?

In this pest-house of the metropolis, and disgrace to the nation, the main thoroughfares are still without common sewers, although the inhabitants have paid exorbitant rates from time immemorial!!!

"O Heaven! That such companions thou'dat unfold,

"And put in every honest hand, a whip,

"To lash the rascals naked through the world."

Unless something be speedily done to allay the growing discontent of the people, retributive justice in her salutary vengeance will commence her operations with the Lamp-Iron and the Halter. SALUS POPULI Lambeth, August 1832

J. W. Peel, Printer, 9, New Cut, Lambeth.

Mr. Peel's early Broadsheets gave way to the circus posters and handbills that formed the vast majority of his output as a printer in New Cut, Lambeth.

One of Mr. Peel's earliest Circus Posters advertised Clarkes New Circus at the Green Dragon, Stepney on Thursday, November 27th 1828. It was printed when J.W.Peele's Office was at 31, New Cut, Lambeth.

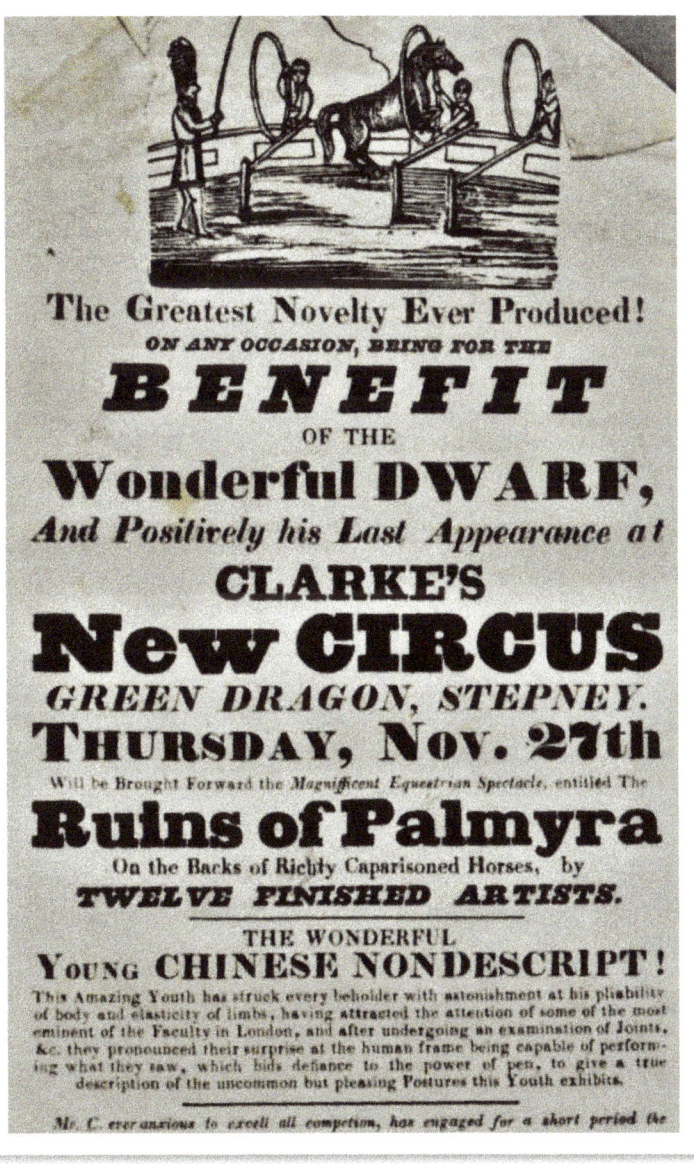

Poster for Clarkes New Circus, 1828

In 1843 Mr. Peel printed a day-bill for Richard Sands American Circus. This was the first American Circus to tour England. From the 28th - 30th November of that year the Circus performed at Stratford upon Avon. A spacious pavilion, advertised as having been made after an entirely new style, was erected on the White Swan Bowling Green. It is Richard Sands who is credited with introducing the typical circus tent to England.

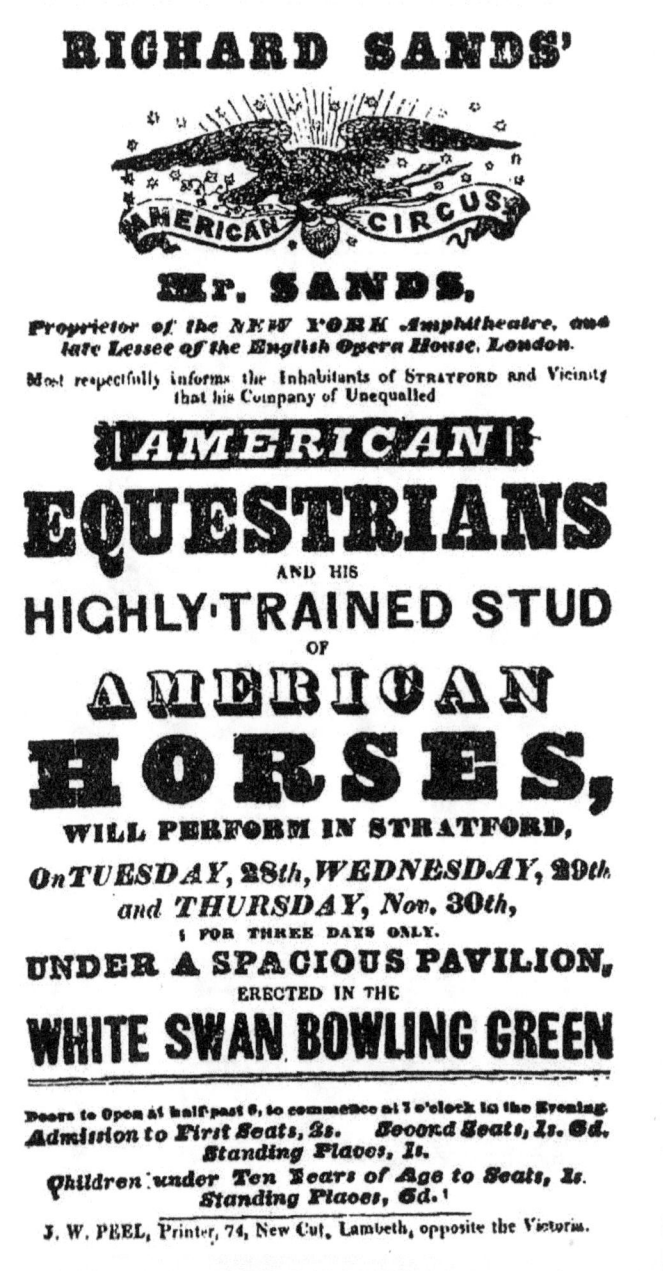

Day Bill for Richard Sands American Circus

In the larger cities, tented circus shows were rare, and performances were presented in permanent buildings. Buildings such as Astley's.

Chapter Thirteen – Permanent Venues – Astleys

It was in an open field "near Glover's Halfpenny Hatch, behind the site of St. John's Church, Waterloo Road at Lambeth that Philip Astley began his career as a showman. Having left the army in 1768. He took a large piece of ground, of a timber-merchant, near Westminster Bridge, on the Surrey side, … and, inclosing it circularly with boarding, erected seats for an audience, with a pent-house roof, covered with canvas, writes Edward W. Brayley, in his book Historical and descriptive accounts of the theatres of London, 1826.

Astley's equestrian school had a circular arena that Astley called his circle, or circus. This would later be known as the ring.

Philip Astley's venture prospered, and he was soon able to erect a partially roofed building which was opened in 1779 as the Amphitheatre Riding House. The entertainments consisted chiefly of equestrian feats, conjuring and fireworks. Establishing the first circus, Astley realized that he needed to bring something new to the performances. Acrobats, rope-dancers and jugglers were added to his equestrian displays. However, Astley's real triumph was identifying the circus's need for clowns. Having obtained a licence in 1783 from the Surrey Justices, he erected a stage and started stage performances.

Astley's Amphitheatre

Location of Astley's Amphitheatre

In 1794 the theatre (then known as the Royal Saloon) with all its properties was burnt down. It was rebuilt on the same site and was opened in the following year as the Amphitheatre of Arts, altered later to Astley's Royal Amphitheatre, under the direction of Philip Astley and his son John. On 2nd September,1803, the theatre was again burnt down, but was rebuilt in 1804 from Astley's own designs. Philip Astley was an enterprising man, with a strong mind and acute understanding. He died on the 20th of October, 1814, in the seventy-third year of his age, at his own residence in Paris, and was buried in the well-known cemetery of Pere la Chaise. His son, who was always termed "Young Astley," died in 1821, in the same bed, in the same house, and was buried in the same grave as his father.

Circus and equestrian performances continued to be successful under Andrew Ducrow who succeeded the Astleys. Edward W. Brayley in 1826, described Astley's at that time. "The prevailing decorations are white, lemon colour, and gold, and the private boxes have hangings of rich crimson. There is one full tier of boxes, and two half tiers at the sides, which range evenly with the front of the gallery: over the half tiers are the gallery slips... The equestrian circle, or ride, which is bounded by a boarded inclosure about four feet in height, painted as stone-work, is forty-four feet in diameter; the area is covered with pulverized saw-dust: the curve of the ride, next the stage, forms the outline of the orchestra, and the remainder that of the pit, which contains fourteen rows of seats, and has a spacious lobby, and a bar for refreshments… The stage, which is probably the largest and most convenient in London, is provided with immense platforms, or floors, rising above each other, and extending entirely across. These are of great strength: the horsemen gallop and skirmish over them, and carriages equal in size and weight to a mail coach may be driven along them. They are so constructed as to be placed and removed, in a short space of time, by manual labour and mechanism. During exhibitions they are masked by romantic scenery, bridges, forts, mountains, and other objects."

Astley's Amphitheatre, Surrey Road

It was in the summer of 1841 that Astley's was burnt down for the third time. Andrew Ducrow died a few months later.

The site of Astley's was then bought by William Batty, the owner of a travelling circus, and Astley's New Royal Amphitheatre of Arts was opened there in 1843. Ten years later it was let to William Cooke on condition that he kept open all the year round. With attractions, such as Shakespeare on horseback, Cooke kept his audiences, but after his departure Astley's rapidly lost its popularity.

Mr. Peel's Printing Office supplied Astley's with posters and handbills from 1836 until 1858. They formed the bulk of Mr. Peel's output, with over one hundred of his Astley posters surviving in collections and archives. Each one giving an insight into the development of the Circus Poster.

Astley's Poster - Last Six Nights of Mazeppa!

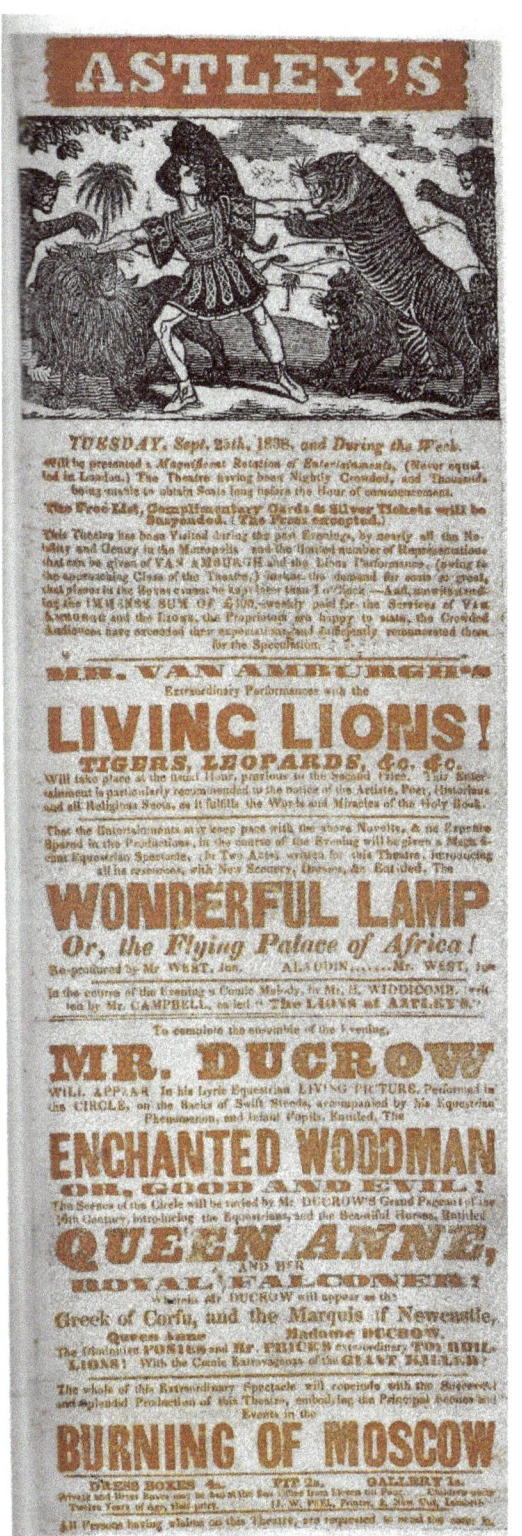 

Two Posters for Astley's

Chapter Fourteen – Batty's

From 1842 to 1853 Astley's Amphitheatre was managed by William Batty, who was by now one of the most successful circus proprietors in Victorian England.

William Batty was an equestrian performer as early as 1828. By 1836 he was operating his own circus, and Pablo Fanque was performing with him in Nottingham as a "rope dancer."

Batty's circus used to travel all over the United Kingdom; in 1838, he was at Newcastle and Edinburgh and, in 1840, at Portsmouth and Southampton.

All the major circus acts of the day performed at Astley's, including W.F. Wallett, one of the most celebrated clowns of the era, and Pablo Fanque who performed there for twelve nights in March 1847. The Illustrated London News reported on Fanque's 1847 run at London's Astley's Amphitheatre:

Mr. Pablo Fanque is an artiste of colour, and his steed ... we have not only never seen surpassed, but never equalled ... Mr. Pablo Fanque was the hit of the evening. The steed in question was Beda, the black mare that Fanque had bought from Batty. That the horse attracted so much attention was testament to Fanque's extraordinary horse training skills.

The paper continued:

"Mr. Pablo has trained [his black mare] to do the most extraordinary feats of the 'manège' an art hitherto considered to belong only to the French and German professors of equitation, and her style certainly far exceeds anything that has ever yet been brought from the Continent...the steed dances to the air, and the band has not to accommodate itself to the action of the horse, as in previous performances of this kind. The grace and facility in shifting time and paces with change of the air, is truly surprising."

Pablo Fanque, born William Darby on 30 March 1810 in Norwich, was a British equestrian performer, entertainer and circus owner. He was in fact the first recorded non-white British circus owner in Britain. His circus was popular in Victorian Britain for 30 years.

Pablo Fanque

Harvest time, 1850. William Batty, procured land some five minutes stroll of the new world-wonder, 'Crystal Palace'. On this land he built and raised, consequently, a curved roofed structure which covered a huge number of onlookers. It had a large arena open to the sky. Batty's Grand National Hippodrome, also known as Batty's Hippodrome, was built to attract audiences from the Great Crystal Palace Exhibition nearby.

Batty's Hippodrome

The Royal Hippodrome was opened in May 1851 with a French troupe brought over from the Hippodrome at Paris. The performances, by and large occurred at night, at a minimal cost of a sixpence. Two brass bands breathed life into the proceedings. Most loved highlights such diversions were a Roman chariot race and a 'victorious race of the Roman consuls', who were represented by the three brothers Debach, each guiding six horses. Other attractions were balloon ascents, and Debach's excursion on the Arienne Ball up and down a narrow inclined plank.

William Batty's Hippodrome opened for a second season in 1852, but a balloon launch went amiss. Its occupants suffered serious injury after the balloon deflated on impact when it crashed into a nearby mansion, just missing the Crystal Palace Exhibition. William Batty stopped all performances at the Hippodrome after the 1852 season, and it shut with the Great Exhibition. William Batty died in 1868, reportedly worth a half a million pounds. He is buried in Kensal Green Cemetery in London.

For the Benefit of Mr. J. W. Peel. Batty's Circus

Poster for Batty's Olympic Arena

Chapter Fifteen – Cornwall's Royal Circus

Along the Marylebone Road, nearly opposite Chapel Street and the entrance to Lisson Grove, was a house bearing the well-known sign of the "Yorkshire Stingo." It was from this tavern that the first pair of London omnibuses were started, July 4th, 1829. They were drawn by three horses, and were such a novelty, that people would come out from their houses in order to see them start. They ran to the Bank and back, and were constructed to carry twenty-two passengers, all inside; the fare was a shilling, or sixpence for half the distance, a sum which included the luxury of the use of a newspaper.

Mr. Peel's posters for Cornwall's Royal Circus give the venue as The Yorkshire Stingo, New Road, and all date to 1843.

Stephen Samwell collaborated with his brother-in-law Henry Cornwall as co-proprietors of Cornwall's Circus. It toured southern counties, Wales, and the Channel Islands in the 1840s. Stephen was born in Mildenhall, Suffolk, to William and Mary Ann Samwell. With the death of William in 1834, Mary Ann took over proprietorship of Samwell's Circus. Stephen, aged only 17, became the Riding Manager. His mother died in 1840.

Stephen and his sister Mary Ann (Henry Cornwall's wife), and at times his brother John, appeared in the shows. Lavater Lee, a famous gymnast and equestrian appeared in Cornwall's Circus in the 1840s.

In 1844 Stephen left Cornwall's Circus and in coming years was engaged with various circuses, touring through England. His speciality was equestrian characters such as the Hero of Waterloo, Mazeppa, The Herculean Horseman, Dick Turpin, and Napoleon Bonaparte. The last records of Stephen as a performer were in 1852. Stephen Samwell died in 1859 he was only 42.

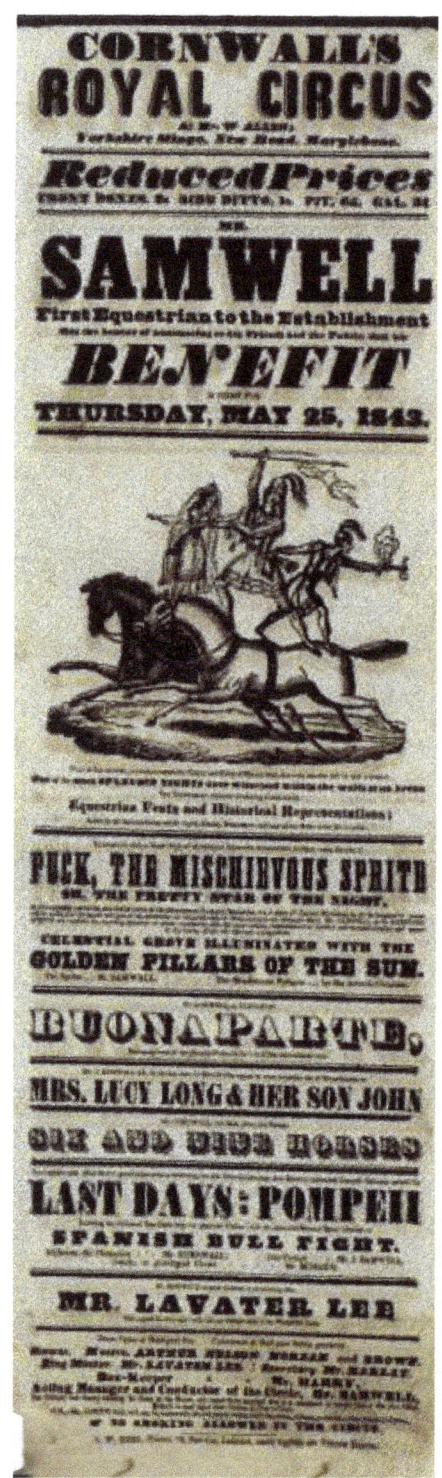

Posters for Cornwall's Royal Circus

Chapter Sixteen – The Royal Surrey Zoological Gardens

From 1844 until 1852 Mr. Peel supplied Playbills and Handbills for the Royal Surrey Zoological Gardens in Newington, Surrey, London. The gardens incorporated a large lake, and occupied about 15 acres to the east side of Kennington Park Road.

Royal Surrey Zoological Gardens

In 1831 the land was acquired by Londoner Edward Cross to be the location of his new Surrey Zoological Gardens. A large circular domed glass conservatory was built in the gardens, with more than 6,000 square feet of glass, to contain separate cages for the animals. The gardens were heavily planted with native and exotic trees and plants, and pavilions were built around the site.

Cross had been the owner of the menagerie at Exeter Exchange in the Strand, and using animals from the Exeter Exchange he set up the Royal Surrey Zoological Gardens to rival the new London Zoo in Regent's Park. The collection expanded in the following years to include lions, tigers, an Indian rhinoceros, an orang-utan, and several giraffes.

From 1837 The Surrey Zoological Gardens were also used for large public entertainments, such as re-enactments of the eruption of Mount Vesuvius, and the Great Fire of London. Even the Storming of Badajoz took place using large painted sets. The Gardens became well known for spectacular firework displays, but when the Great Exhibition took place at the Crystal Palace in 1851, the gardens suffered from the intense competition.

Cross retired in 1844, and he died in Kennington in 1854. His wife, Mary, predeceased him. After Cross's death, Surrey Zoological Gardens were acquired by a company. They let the zoo become run down and then the animals were sold off in 1856. The Surrey Zoological Gardens later became the Surrey Music Hall.

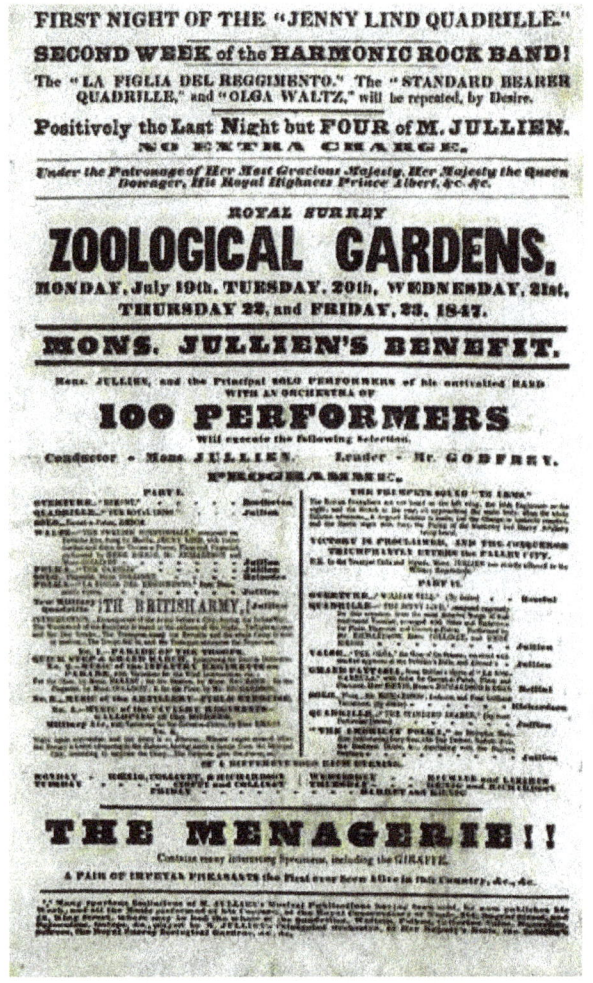

Handbill for The Surrey Zoological Gardens

Chapter Seventeen – Vauxhall Gardens

Poster for Vauxhall Gardens

One of the main venues for public entertainment in London from the mid-seventeenth century to the mid-nineteenth century were the Vauxhall Gardens. A public park in Kennington, on the south bank of the River Thames, London, the Gardens drew large crowds. Admission was charged for its attractions. A writer at the time wrote: "Entrance into the gardens, which extends over about eleven acres, is admirably calculated to enhance their extraordinary effect on the first view. We step at once from the passages into a scene of enchantment, such as in our young days opened upon our eyes as we pored over the magical pages of the 'Arabian Nights."

With its paths noted for romantic assignations, Vauxhall's points of interest included the rococo "Turkish tent". Lavish chinoiserie style decoration made the Turkish Tent one of Vauxhall's most popular attractions. Chinoiserie style was a feature of several buildings built around the gardens. Tightrope walkers, hot-air balloon ascents, concerts and fireworks provided the visitors with diverse entertainments. In 1817, the Battle of Waterloo was re-enacted, using 1,000 soldiers.

Forster's "Life of Dickens," recalls that one famous night, the 29th of June, 1849, Dickens went there with Judge Talfourd, Stanfield, and Sir Edwin Landseer. The 'Battle of Waterloo' formed part of the entertainment on that occasion. "We were astounded," writes Mr. Forster, "to see pass in immediately before us, in a bright white overcoat, the 'great duke' himself, with Lady Douro on his arm, the little Lady Ramsay by his side, and everybody cheering and clearing the way for him. That the old hero enjoyed it all there could be no doubt, and he made no secret of his delight in 'Young Hernandez, but the battle was undeniably tedious,; and it was impossible not to sympathise with the repeatedly and audibly expressed wish of Talfourd that 'the Prussians would come up!'" It must have been one of the old duke's last appearances in a place of amusement, as he lived only three years longer.

The Gardens closed in 1840 after its owners suffered bankruptcy, but re-opened a year later. Although Vauxhall Gardens changed hands again, it was permanently closed in 1859. In the autumn of that year there was an announcement: "The well-known theatre, orchestra, dancing-platform, firework-gallery, fountains, statues, vases, &c.," would be sold by auction. There were, in all, 274 lots. Many of them sold for the lowest price.

Mr. Peel's posters for Vauxhall Gardens, listing the entertainments, span the years 1842 to 1851. His 1846 poster advertising a concert by Signor Negri, and 'Mr. Ducrow and his magnificent stud of horses and ponies and the entire company of Astley's late theatre'. In fact, Astley's Amphitheatre in Lambeth burnt down three times. After the final time in 1841, Astley's Rotunda was rebuilt in the grounds of Vauxhall Gardens, for equestrian events.

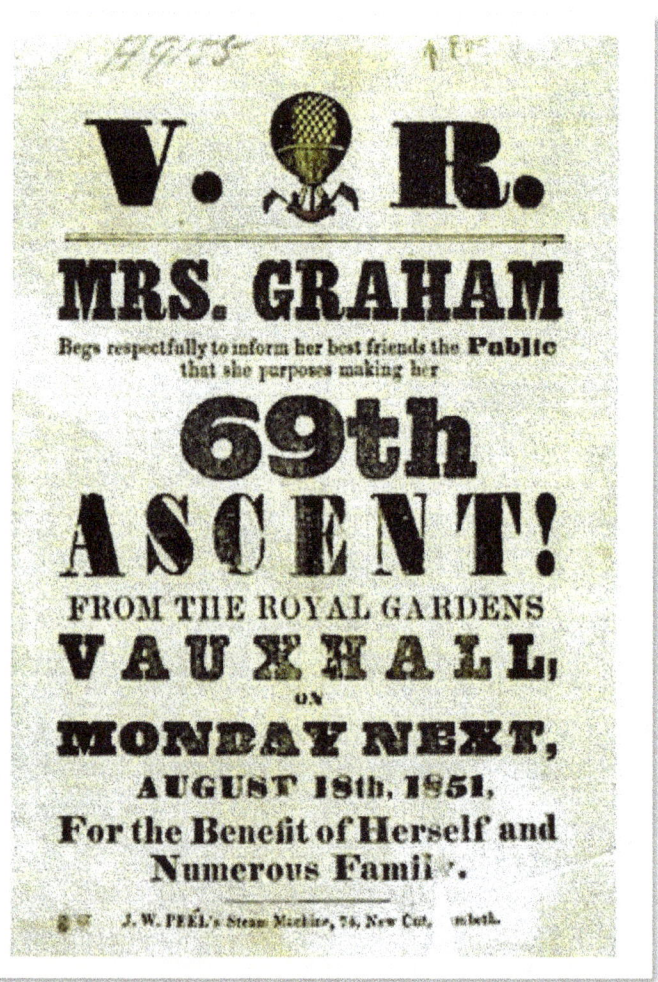

Poster for Mrs. Graham's 69th Ascent from Vauxhall Gardens

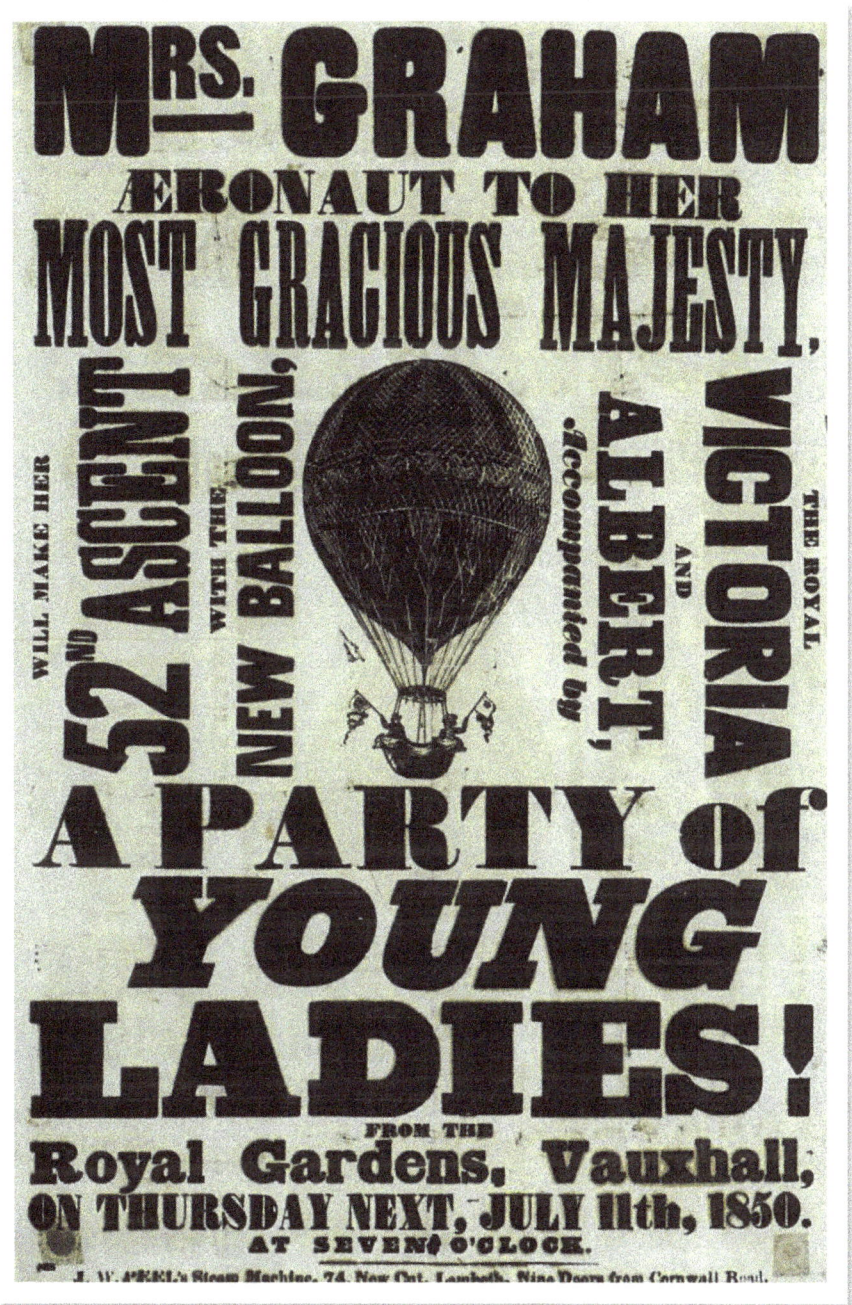

Poster for Mrs. Graham's Ascent from Vauxhall Gardens 1850

Chapter Eighteen – The Victoria Theatre

Dating back to 1816 The Victoria Theatre is one of the oldest theatre buildings in London.

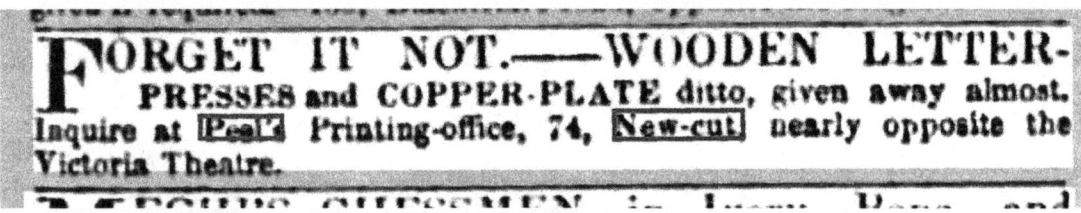

Advertisement – Morning Advertiser 20th October 1842

When John Websdale Peel moved to New Cut in 1823, he lived and worked immediately opposite the theatre. A fact that he never fails to mention in his newspaper advertisements. For example: The Era, Sunday 5 December 1858

Steam - Steam: Forget it Not

John Peel. Printer 74 New Cut, Lambeth, opposite the Victoria Theatre.

Established in 1818 as the Royal Coburg Theatre, under the patronage of Princess Charlotte. She had married the Prince of Saxe-Coburg, and the theatre was named, as a compliment to the princess. The Royal Coburg was quickly a success and many West End Theatre actors performed there including Edmund Kean, who played there in 1831 for a fee of £50 a night, a huge sum at the time.

When the Theatre was redecorated in 1833 and reopened on the 1st of July of that year it was renamed the Royal Victoria Theatre, having secured the patronage of Victoria, Duchess of Kent.

Paganini the famous Italian violinist, guitarist and composer, had his farewell performance at the Victoria Theatre on June the 17th 1834.

On 15th April 1831 an application for a Printing Press at The Royal Coburg Theatre was tendered by George Bolwell Davidge. Davidge, was the actor-manager of The Coburg Theatre for seven years from 1826 to 1833. John Websdale Peel had signed Davidge's application for a printing press at the Coburg; in 1833 he printed a poster for the Royal Victoria Theatre (late Coburg). It is no surprise that Mr. Peel and Mr. Davidge got on well, as Davidge was originally apprenticed to a printer. Then living and working at No.9 New Cut, John Websdale Peel was four doors away from Davidge at no.5 Charlotte Terrace, New Cut.

On 31 January 1842 in Davidge Terrace, Walcot Place, Lambeth, George Bolwell Davidge died. He was in his 50th year. His will contained numerous generous legacies.

Mr. Peel's posters for The Victoria Theatre cover the twenty five year period from 1833 to 1858.

Poster for Victoria Theatre 1st July 1833

Jonathan Joy

Chapter Nineteen – Cremorne Gardens

Poster for Cremorne Gardens

When Cremorne House was first opened to the public in 1831 it was as a sports stadium. Then in 1845 Thomas Bartlett Simpson, a hotelkeeper and entrepreneur, took over management of the gardens. Although he may not have initiated the opening as pleasure grounds, he seems to have been the one responsible for their success.

Cremorne Gardens was opened to the public in 1846 and within a few years became established as a popular feature of London's summer season. With its annual programme of events being welcomed by the press each May. It took advantage of the greater number of people with leisure-time in the mid-19th century. Admission remained 1s. to enter the grounds, making it relatively affordable to the general public.

Cremorne Gardens occupied a large site running between the Thames and the King's Road. It could be entered from the north gate on Kings Road or another by the Cremorne Pier on the river. Noisy and colourful the pleasure gardens featuring restaurants, entertainments, dancing and balloon ascents. A poster printed by Mr. Peel survives. Dated 20 May 1850 it advertises Royal Cremorne Gardens and its entertainments.

The artist James Abbott McNeill Whistler painted several nocturnes of Cremorne Gardens between 1872 and 1877. He was a resident of Cheyne Walk, a mere few hundred yards from the Gardens. His painting Cremorne Gardens No 2 is full of fashionable figures. The gardens also provided the setting for Nocturne in Black and Gold: the Fire-wheel, and the Falling Rocket of c.1874.

In the 1850s Simpson was able to secure court and aristocratic patronage, but by the 1860s Cremorne was attracting criticism. As a place of entertainment bringing together a wide range of social groups the Gardens drew sustained attacks from the Chelsea vestry, local residents, and moralists from a wider area. Cremorne Gardens finally became so great an annoyance to some of the more influential residents in the neighbourhood that a renewal of its licence was refused, and the gardens closed in 1877. The site was soon built over. The name surviving in Cremorne Road.

Chapter Twenty – The Surrey Theatre

Mr. Peel's posters for the Surrey Theatre are from the 1850s. The poster for 27 February 1850 advertising Richard Dewhurst, Clown of All Clowns. Dewhurst was a circus clown who was also an accomplished 'leaper', which was an attraction of ground acrobats in the early 19th century, and a popular amateur sport in the north of England. In contemporary publicity Dewhurst was described as being able to leap over 14 feet high, over ten horses, and through six balloons. Richard Dewhurst's final Benefit performance at Batty's Circus, Westminster Road, was on 23rd February 1842.

First opened under the title of the "Royal Circus and Equestrian Philharmonic Academy." The Surrey Theatre, London began life in 1782 as the Royal Circus and Equestrian Philharmonic Academy, one of the many circuses that provided entertainment of both horsemanship and drama (hippodrama). It stood in Blackfriars Road, near the junction with Westminster Bridge Road, just south of the River Thames.

The Circus was destroyed by fire in August, 1805, it was soon rebuilt and re-opened at Easter, 1806. Three years later and a Mr, Ellison became the lessee. Elliston introduced several of Shakespeare's plays, and endeavoured to raise the character of the house. On the 5th of March, 1810, in a petition to Parliament he tried, but failed to introduce "such entertainments of music and action as are commonly called pantomimes and ballets, together with operatic or musical pieces, accompanied with dialogue.

The petition, however, was rejected, on the ground that it would, 'go far to alter the whole principle upon which theatrical entertainments are at present regulated within the metropolis and twenty miles round.'

By 1829 the theatre's fortunes had changed, Douglas Jerrold's melodrama Black-Eyed Susan, with T. P. Cooke as William, the nautical hero, ran for over 300 nights, which was extraordinarily successful for the time. Elliston made his last appearance at this theatre on 24 June 1831, twelve days before he died.

Mr. Osbaldiston then took over and, among other plays, produced the Murder at the Roadside Inn, which ran for 260 nights. Productions of Dickens dramas, among others, followed. Ira Aldridge, the first successful black actor, appeared here in the 1840s.

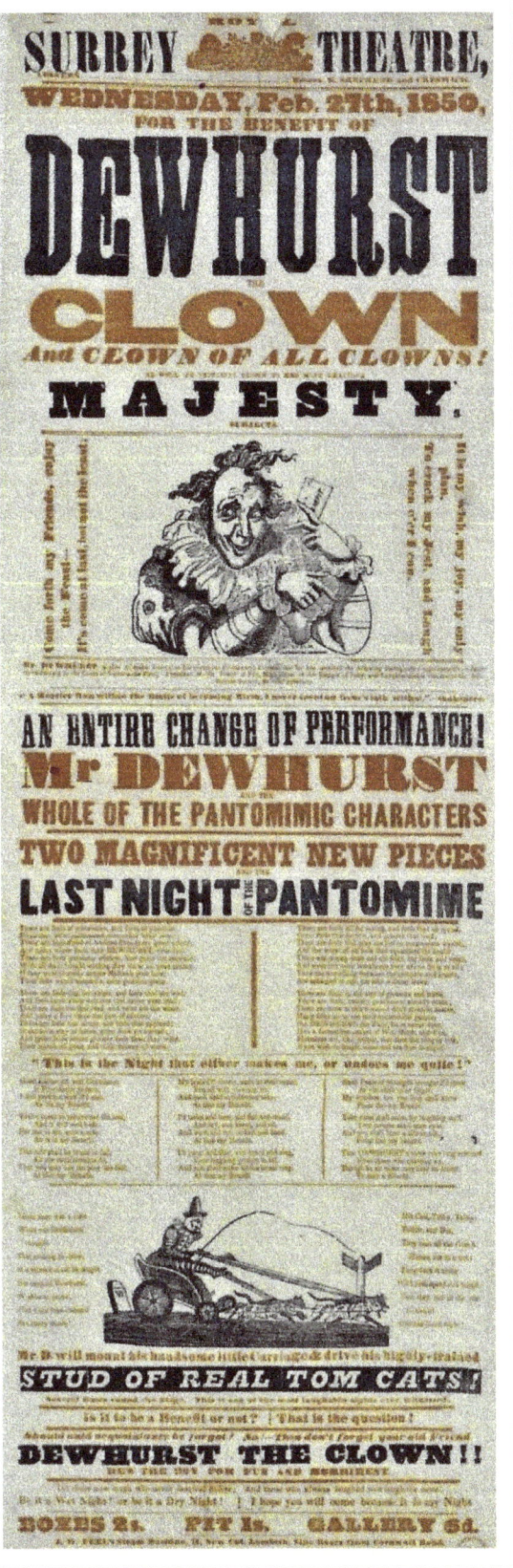

*Poster for The Surrey Theatre,
February 27th 1850*

Chapter Twenty-One – The Grecian Saloon

Handbill for The Grecian Saloon 1842

Poster for The Grecian Saloon 1843

Mr Peel's Poster

The Royal Grecian Theatre was a theatre on the corner of City Road and Shepherdess Walk, in Shoreditch, north London. Originally built in 1821 as the Eagle tavern, by 1832 a pavilion had been built in its grounds known as the Grecian Saloon. The saloon was rebuilt in 1841 and became a proper theatre.

Between July 1841 and November 1843, Mr. Peel printed both Handbills and Posters for The Grecian Saloon. Advertising all kinds of entertainments, from religious events to conjuring and equestrian performances.

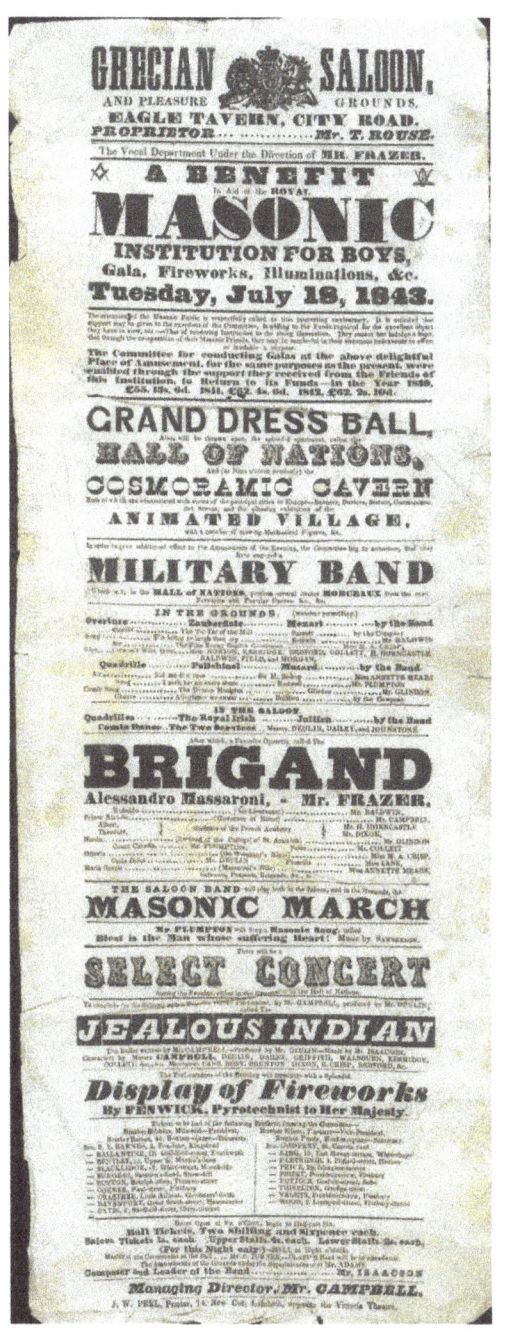
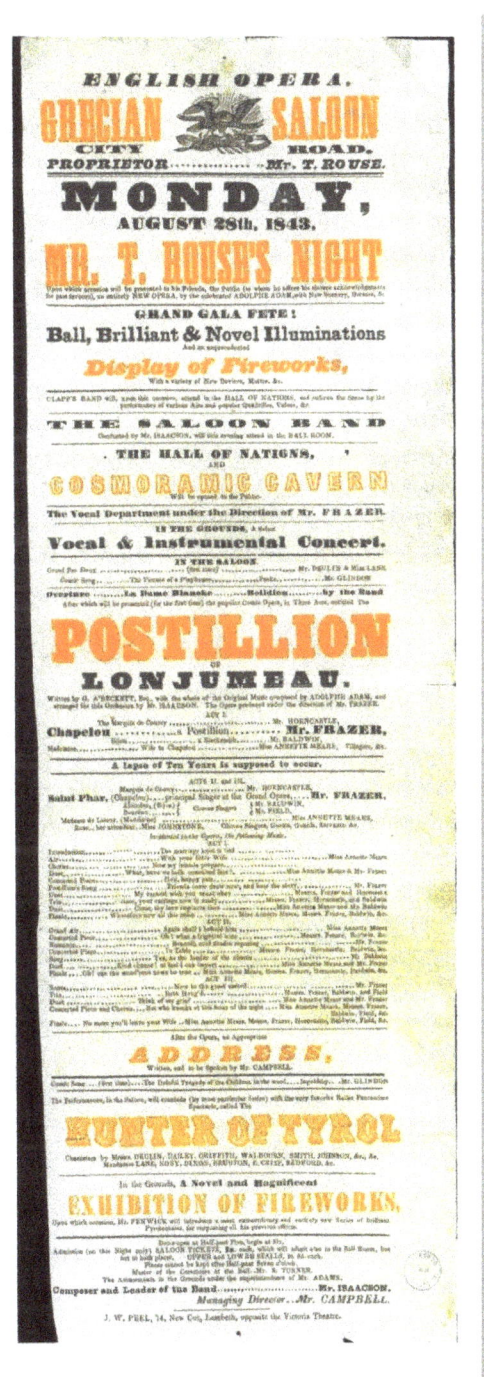

Chapter Twenty-Two – Travelling Circuses-Clarkes

In 1828-1829 Clarke's Troupe set up on ground behind the Green Dragon, Stepney. The same piece of ground mentioned at the THE OLD BAILEY on 10th April 1828.

JOHN BLAKES. I am a labourer. I left a male ass in the possession of Mr. Pottinger, at the Green Dragon at Stepney, for 1s. 6d. a week, the latter end of August; I went there on the 23d of December and paid a fortnight's keep; it was missed on the 24th, but I did not go again till the 30th, and when I went on the green, behind the Green Dragon, it was gone - I found it on the 18th of February in the possession of Mr. Smith; the man whom I bought it of stopped it coming from the West India Docks.

Mr. Peel's posters advertising Clarkes Circus at the Green Dragon are the earliest known circus posters printed by him.

Box 2s. Pit 1s. Gal. (with seats) 6d. The doors to be opened at six o'clock and to begin precisely at 7. Good Fires are constantly kept. CIRCUS TICKETS to be TAKEN at the BAR. Ladies and Gentlemen taught the Art of Riding and Managing the Horse.

J. W. PEELE, Printer, 31, New Cut, Lambeth

Following Mr. Clarke's performance, a Miss Clarke was to balance with and without a pole on the tightrope. After her, an eight-year old boy called Benjamin Saffery did slack-rope vaulting. Clarke supposedly served as the model for Sleary, the circus owner in Charles Dickens novel Hard Times.

Another poster proclaims:

NEW CIRCUS, BACK OF THE GREEN DRAGON, STEPNEY, WILL OPEN FOR A SHORT TIME, THIS EVENING AND UNTIL FURTHER NOTICE. MR. CLARKE, (The first time of his Extensive Company of Equestrians having the honor to appear here) presumes on the liberty of intimating to the Ladies, Gentlemen, & the Visitors in general that it is his determination, during his short stay, to introduce a chaste scientific, and rational entertainment, which will be conducted with the utmost decorum possible to be obtained during his stay. Being at all times averse to puffing, would rather exceed the bill than, by a country plan, force a disappoint-ment on his patrons; and pledges his word that, all and everything inserted in the bills will be punctually introduced. He further observes, that his Performers are of the FIRST TALENT in their departments.

The whole to conclude with the Comic Extravaganza, called Jeremiah the Lean Box 2s. Pit 1s. Gal. (with seats) 6d. The doors to be opened at six o'clock and to begin precisely at 7. Good Fires are constantly kept. CIRCUS TICKETS to be TAKEN at the BAR. Ladies and Gentlemen taught the Art of Riding and Managing the Horse. J. W. PEELE, Printer, 31, New Cut, Lambeth.

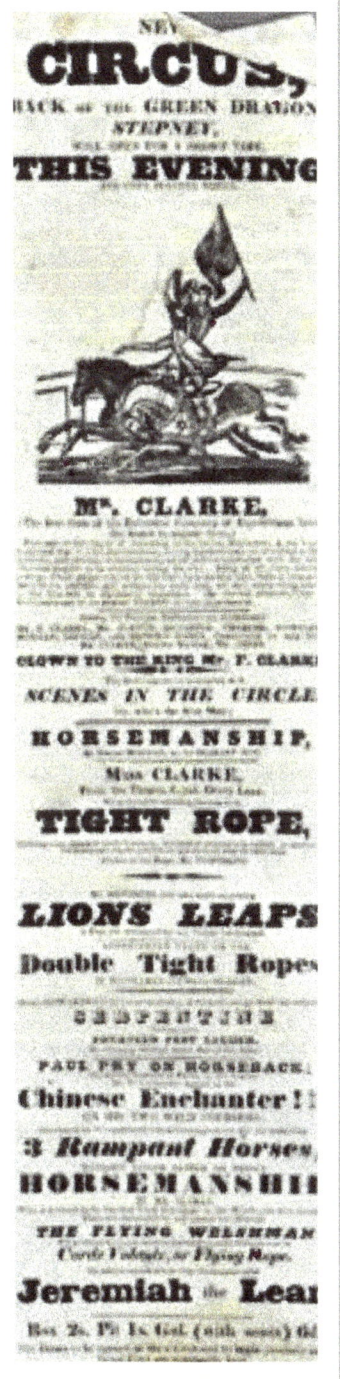

Poster Clarkes Circus 1828

Chapter Twenty-Three – Cookes

One of the more celebrated "circus families". Cooke's Circus consisted of family and extended family all having some expertise in equestrian acts, and as tumblers, strongmen and acrobats. Primarily an equestrian show, over half the acts involved horses, based for a time in the 1830s at Cooke's (Royal) Equestrian Circus in Great Windmill Street. Cooke's Circus mainly travelled around cities and the large towns of England and Scotland. In fact Cooke's Circus was one of the first circuses to follow the example of Astley's Circus by touring abroad. The circus travelling to Spain and Portugal in 1816.

Following a visit from King William IV and Queen Adelaide, in the autumn of 1830, the company received the name "Royal Circus" and held the name Cooke's Royal Circus (1780–1912), for the rest of their existence.

When Mr. Cooke, became a manager of Astley's Amphitheatre, he had the idea of producing Shakespeare's historical plays. By bringing Richard III to Astley's for the first time, Richard was seen on the stage, surrounded by his staff on horseback, and himself mounted on that famous steed, 'White Surrey.' Encouraged by this success, Astley's company next appeared in Henry IV, and Macbeth.

Cookes Circus staged one very dramatic equestrian show called "Mazeppa", based on a poem by Byron. This concept was borrowed from Andrew Ducrow's show Mazeppa of 1831. In 1846 a similar style of show was based on the life of Dick Turpin.

Thomas Cooke died in 1866 in London and is buried in Kensal Green Cemetery. The grave is highly unusual, carrying a statue of a horse "mourning".

Mr. Peel printed a unique poster for Cookes Circus for the Friday Evening performance of 25 February 1830. The striking woodcut image showing Mr. Wells, the Antipodean Clown with the word CLOWN printed upside-down.

Cookes Circus Poster 1830

Chapter Twenty-Four – Price and Powell's Circus

Irishman, Thomas Price (1813-1877) began his circus career in London at the age of 13, where he showed great promise as a clown in the Ducrow circus. He is said to have been able to make 70 leaps in a row.

In 1835 he performed at the James Ryan's Royal Circus, opposite William Powell and Henry Hengler. The three must have put their heads together, because they decided to create their own circus. In 1841 they founded the Price and Powell Royal Circus in London. To begin with, it was not very successful because it closed its doors in 1843.

Price tried again. Partnered by the American Levi North they founded Price and North's Equestrian Company.

Finally, he decided to open his own circus on Devonport Street, London, in 1845.

Lack of success, and perhaps the search for fortune found Thomas Price in Madrid in 1847. Here success was huge, and his soon became the most important circus in Madrid. Mr. Price died suddenly on August 22, 1877.

William Powell was an equestrian. Born in 1815, in Edinburgh, he had been with Batty's Circus as a teenager. From 1841-1843 he was co-owner of Price and Powell's Royal Circus, then, when the partnership was dissolved on April18 1843 he became sole owner. The new Powell's Royal Circus played Hammersmith and Stepney. In August and September 1843 the circus was in Dover. And in October they performed in Canterbury. By December

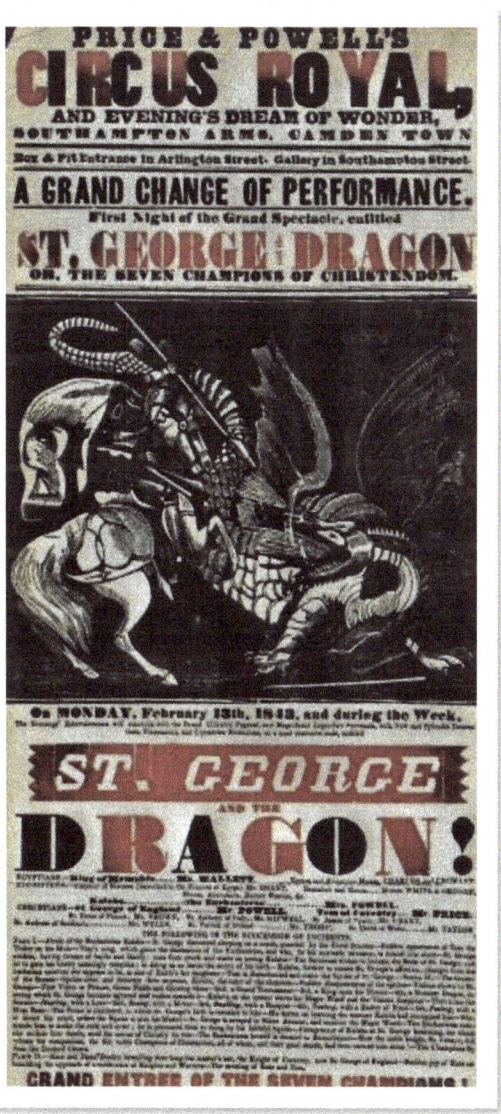

Poster for Price and Powell's Circus

1843 they were back in London Street, Greenwich, but Mr. Powell had been experiencing financial trouble for some time even before Greenwich and finally closed the doors on Monday 19th February 1844.

With dates of 1842 and 1843, Mr. Peel's posters for Price and Powell's Circus display wood cuts of George and the Dragon, and Mr. Powell driving his Real Cats, Four in Hand, several times around the circle.

In 1843 it was Mr. Peel who printed a day-bill for the first American Circus to tour England. Advertising a three day performance by Richard Sands American Circus at the White Swan Bowling Green, Stratford upon Avon from 28-30 November.

Later he promoted Howes and Cushing's Great United States Circus when they toured the country in 1858 and opened at the Alhambra Palace, Leicester Square, London.

 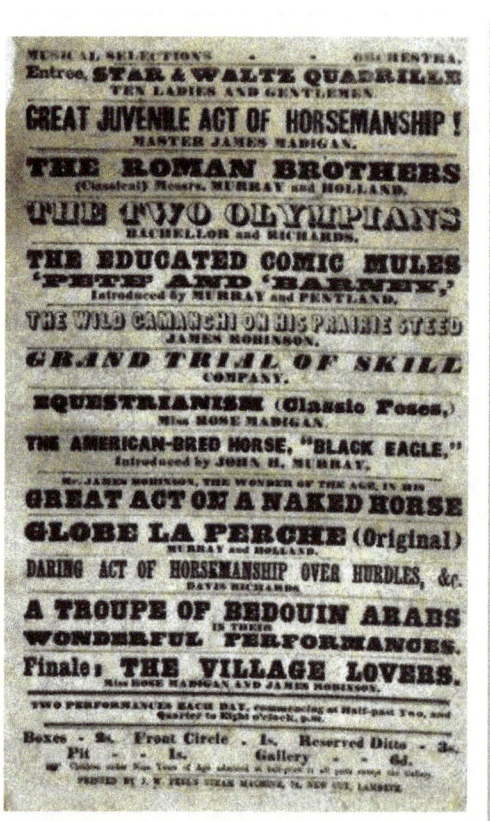

Handbill for Howes and Cushing's Great United States Circus

Price and North's American Circus

Levi North, the equestrian, was the first American headliner to appear in London, making him an ambassador for the western school of riding. Audiences in Europe were astonished that a rider from the States had so much ability. Levi North's journey to London is well documented. North's voyage from America to Liverpool took twenty-four days, and then to London, by stagecoach, another three.

When Levi North arrived in London he had an interview with the great Andrew Ducrow, proprietor of Astley's amphitheatre. Engaged by Ducrow, North arranged for a special vaulting board to be made. In performing on such a board, the performer could turn somersaults consecutively, his ability being measured by the number of turns he made.

A contest was arranged at Astley's. Rehearsals began on 30 June 1838. North, then aged 24 was paired against the Englishman Thomas Price. North did thirty-one somersaults, increasing to thirty-two on 2 July, the first performance of the contest. Price did fewer. Ducrow had the two vaulting boards set side by side, and with British and American flags set up to enhance the rivalry aspect of the performance. The contest went on for twelve nights, in only one of which Price was the winner. North reached his zenith at forty-four somersaults on 19 July, to the audiences' amazement.

Thomas Price and Levi North had become stars overnight, and proved their status as two of the leading performers in England at that time. Former rivals, they joined together in 1843 to put Price & North's Circus on tour. At the season's end North returned home to America.

Working for Price & North's British and American Equestrian Company, Mr. Peel had an interesting commission. He was to produce stock posters, with the date and venue to be filled in whenever needed. Although the posters carry no date, they must have been printed in early 1843 as Price & North's British and American Equestrian Company only toured for that year.

Poster for Price & North's British & American Equestrian Company

Poster for Price & North's British & American Equestrian Company

Handbill for Howes & Cushing American Circus

Howes and Cushing's Great United States Circus

In 1856 Seth Howes and Joseph Cushing forged a partnership in the United States.

They left America and sailed to Liverpool, landing on 25th March 1857. With them they had 72 horses and 50 performers and assistants.

The Circus travelled the country, eventually opening at the Alhambra Palace, Leicester Square, London. Here they performed before Queen Victoria and the Royal Family who often attended circus performances. Recording in her journal, " a very varied and wonderful performance" with " excellent riding...a man who lept over seven horses", and " a very clever black horse which did all sorts of things."

Chapter Twenty-Five – Exhibitions and Displays

The posters and handbills that formed the vast majority of Mr. Peel's output as a printer in New Cut, Lambeth were designed to call attention to a venue or event. A poster had clear advantages in relation to other advertising opportunities in nineteenth century London. The speed with which Mr. Peel's posters could be printed. The size of the poster, the bold typography, the colour and the striking visual design using wood engravings, all helped to inform the public of the show and where and when it was taking place.

Mr. Peel supplied posters and handbills on a regular basis to venues such as Astley's and Batty's Royal Hippodrome. However, all too often Mr. Peel's printing business was called on to provide one poster for one venue and one event. Of which there are numerous surviving examples:

A Handbill - Exhibition of Part of the Wreck of The Royal George. On August 29th 1782, the 100-gun warship HMS Royal George sunk whilst lying at anchor off Spithead. The death toll was huge, with estimates varying between six hundred and one thousand people drowned.

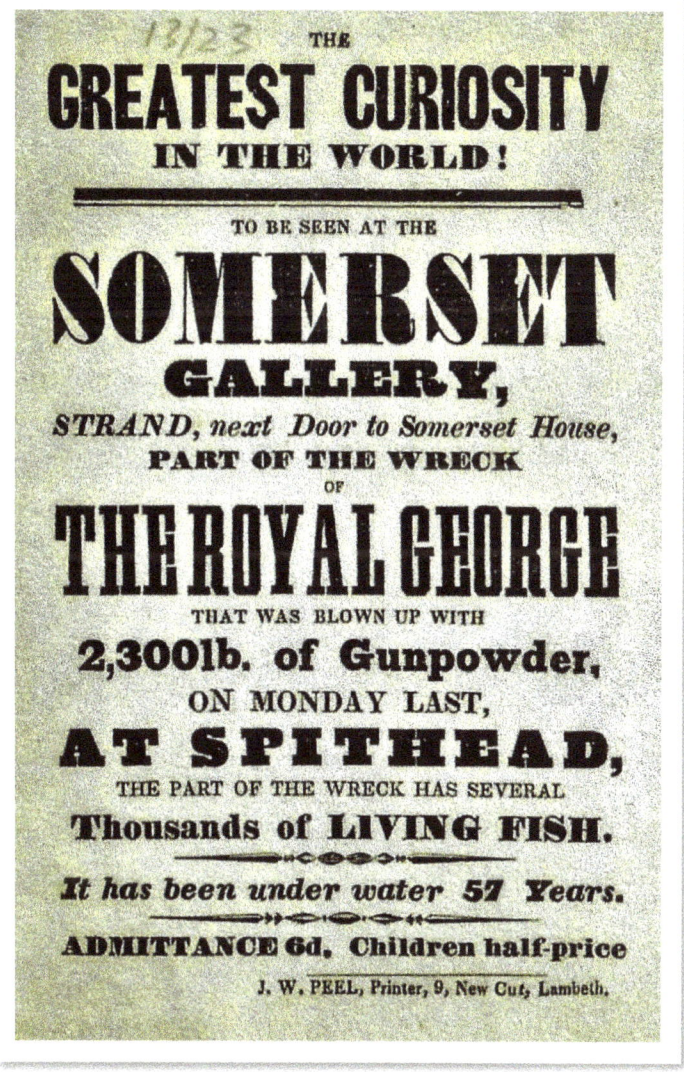

Handbill for The Royal George Wreck Exhibition

Eventually in May 1840, the wreck was blown up, but not before most of her cannon and some of her timbers had been saved.

Mr. Peel's poster advertised Part of the wreck of The Royal George, to be seen at The Somerset Gallery, Strand, next door to Somerset House.

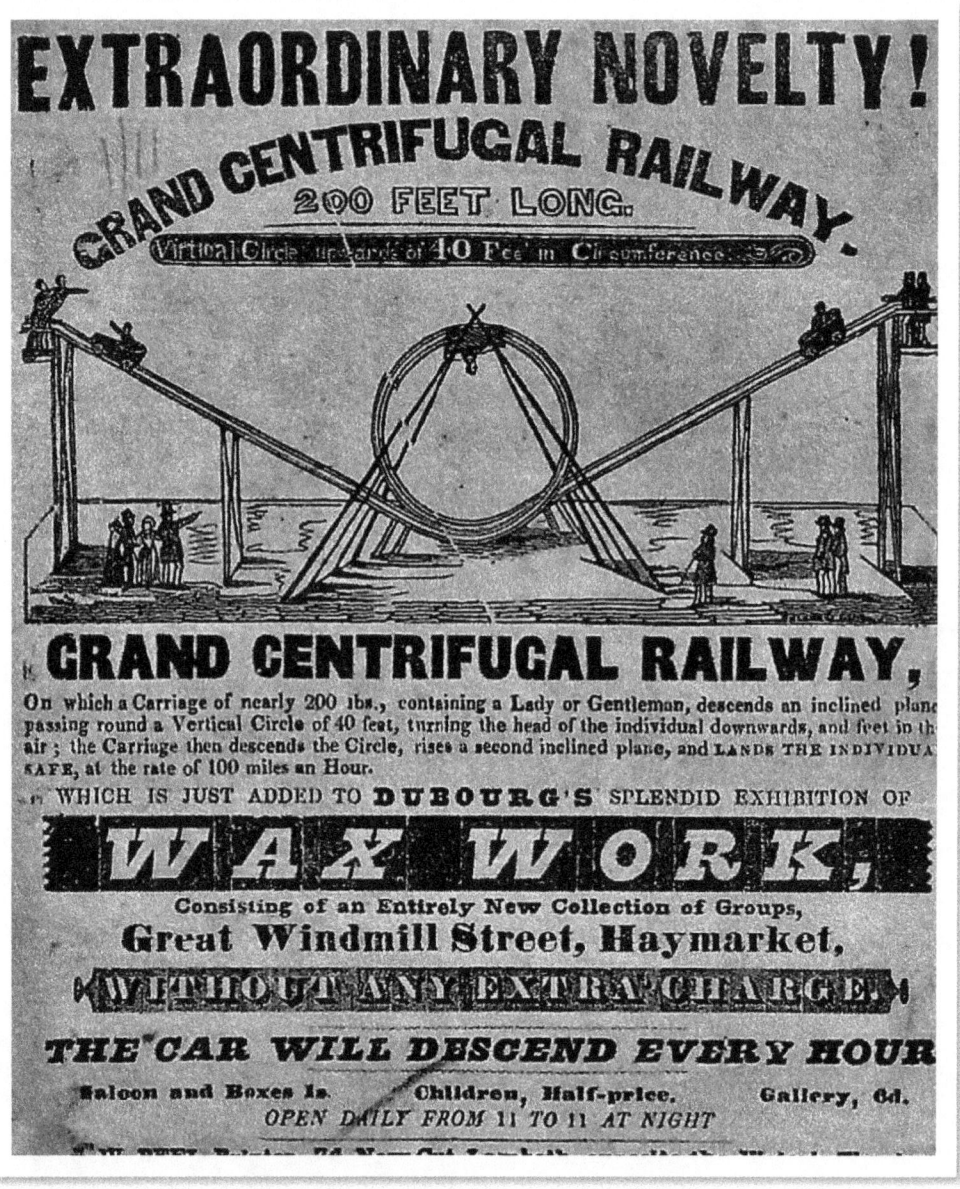

Poster for the Grand Centrifugal Railway,

A Poster - Saturday, September 24, 1842

Extraordinary Novelty!

Grand Centrifugal Railway, 200 feet long, on which a Carriage of nearly 200lbs. containing a Lady or Gentleman, descends an inclined plane, passing round a Vertical Circle of 40 feet, turning the head of the individual downwards, and feet in the air; the Carriage then Descends the Circle, rises a second inclined plane, and lands the individual safe, at the rate of 100 miles an hour; which is just added to Dubourg's splendid Exhibition of Mechanical Figures, ... Great Windmill street, Haymarket. The Car will descend every hour.

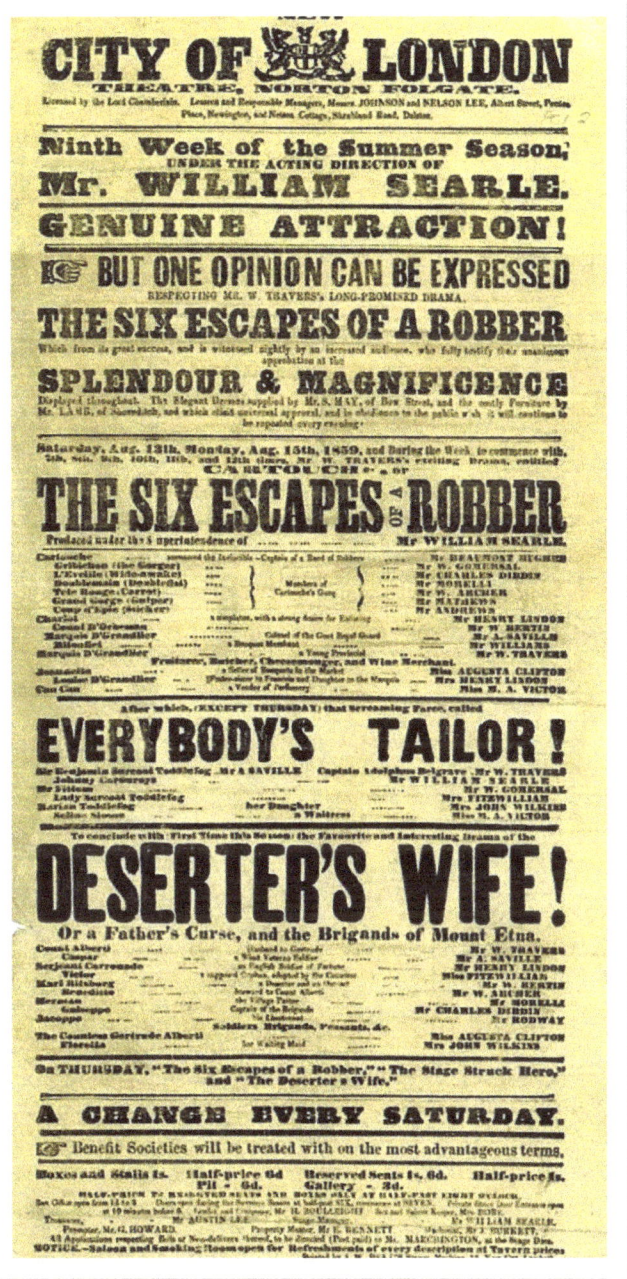

Poster of City of London Theatre, Norton Holgate

A Poster - City of London Theatre. Norton Folgate Monday 13 August 1859.

Advertising The Deserter's Wife or a Father's Curse and the Brigands of Mount Etna.

Easter Monday the 27th of March 1837 and the Theatre opened with the name The Royal City of London Theatre. Its first major production was Edward Stirling's version of Dicken's 'Pickwick Club' on Tuesday the 28th of March 1837.

On the 7th of October 1844, the Theatre was reopened, after being redecorated. The City of London Theatre was later taken over by Nelson Lee and John Johnson in 1848. It was to prove a most successful period. It is thought that they were the only managers who ever made the City Theatre pay. Nelson Lee's first pantomime at the Theatre, under his own management, was entitled, 'Love, War and Peace'.

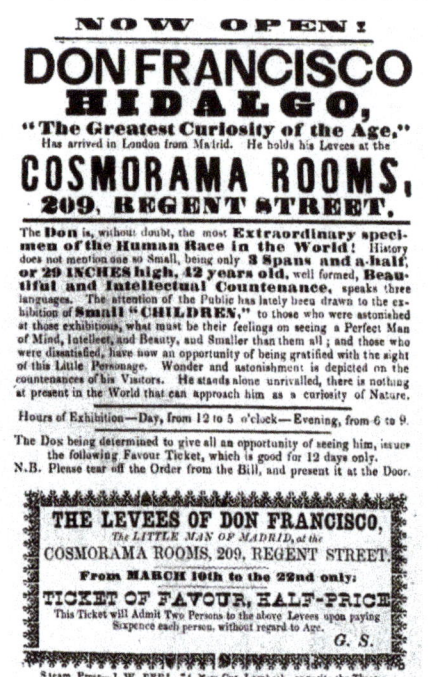

Don Francisco Hidalgo

A Poster - The Poster for the Cosmorama Rooms shows a portrait of Don Francisco Hidalgo. The Marquis of Lilliput: Don Francisco Hidalgo whole-length, standing in front of a table, looking towards the right, wearing coat open over waistcoat, holding cane in his right hand, left hand holding paper inscribed 'One fourth the size of Life'; within red rectangular border with flower vase on each side. Printed by: J W Peel.

The COSMORAMA occupied Nos. 207 and 209, REGENT STREET. Intended primarily for exhibiting views of remarkable scenes in different parts of the world, but were chiefly used as ordinary exhibition rooms. The subjects being changed every two or three months.

A Playbill - 103 Drury Lane, an exhibition of a Bearded Lady. January 22, 1853

Madame Fortunne, was born Josephine Boisdechêne in Versoix, Switzerland. She was born hairy. Reputedly had a two-inch beard at the age of eight, and at the age of fourteen she began to tour Europe, often accompanied by her father. When in Paris she met painter Fortune Clofullia and eventually married him. She toured with P. T. Barnum's "American Museum" as Josephine Clofullia.

In July 1853 Mr. William Charr took Clofullia to court, claiming that she was actually a man and an impostor. During the

Madame Fortunne

case doctors examined her and verified that she was a female and the case was eventually dismissed. By hearsay it has been suspected that Barnum arranged the whole matter himself as a publicity stunt. She died in 1875 aged 48.

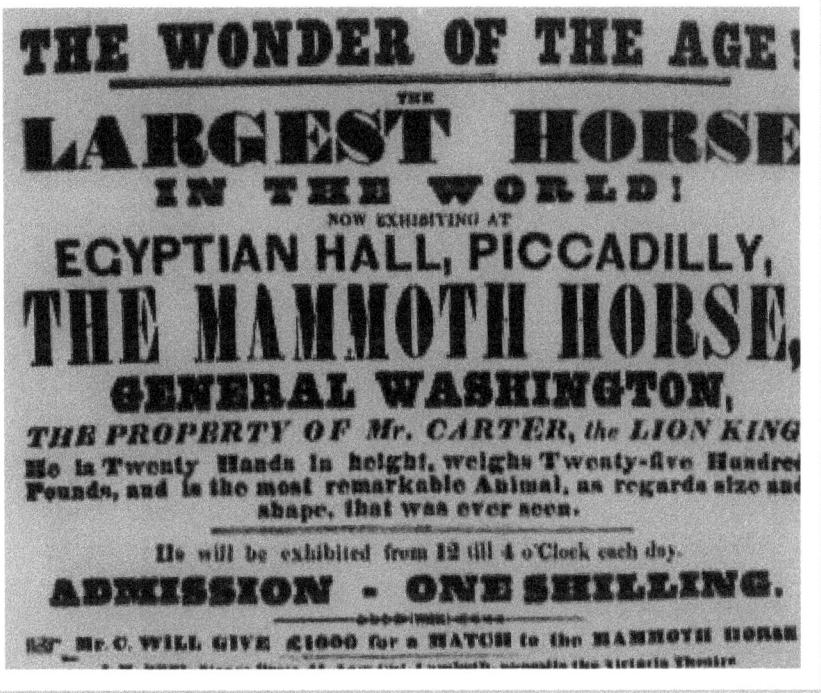

The Egyptian Hall. Largest Horse in the World

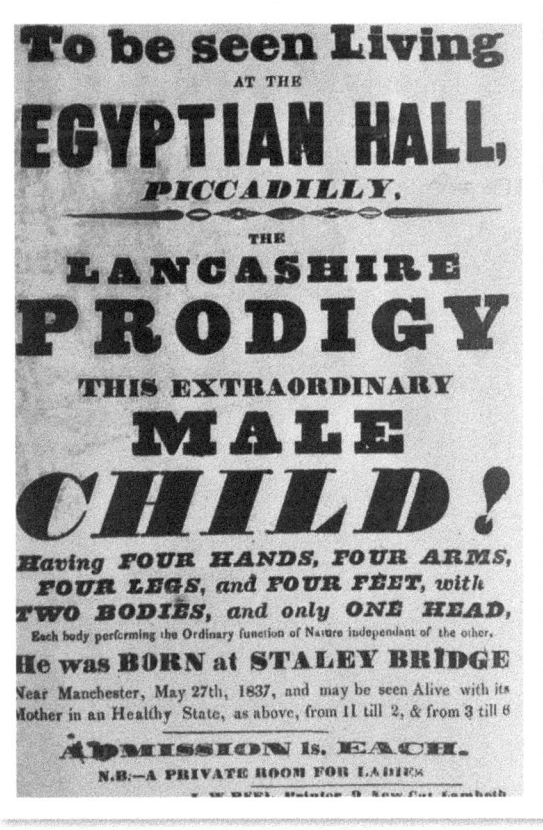

The Egyptian Hall. The Lancashire Prodigy

Handbills - The Lancashire Prodigy: The Egyptian Hall. August 1838, and

The Largest Horse in the World. The Mammoth Horse. The Egyptian Hall. Piccadilly.

The Egyptian Hall, (Bullock's Museum, or London Museum), Piccadilly became a major venue for the exhibiting of works of art; it had the advantage of being almost the only London venue able to exhibit really large works.

It was the first building in England to be influenced by the Egyptian style, and was a considerable success, with an exhibition of Napoleonic era relics in 1816 including Napoleon's carriage taken at Waterloo being seen by about 220,000 visitors.

A Poster - Grand Exhibitions of Art. Adjoining the Adelaide Gallery, Strand

GRAND EXHIBITIONS OF ART. ADJOINING THE Adelaide Gallery, Strand. This Superb and Matchless Exhibition defies all competition being the only one in existence having been collected together at the Cost of many Thousands of Pounds. A LARGE MECHANICAL ELEPHANT AND BELL RINGER, The Size of Life, which rings 500 changes on 10 Silver Bells. INTERESTING AUTOMATON LADY ORGANIST Size of Life, mechanically playing the Organ with its Fingers. GORGEOUS TEMPLE OF FOUNTAINS. With Falls of Water ascending and descending from the Mouths of Dolphins, Tritons, MAGNIFICENT PEARL EATERS, Extremely gorgeous and richly set with many Thousands of Stones, Gems, and said to have cost £20,000. LARGE MECHANICAL SERPENTS AND PALM TREES. Twelve Feet High! Matchless SINGING BIRD in a CAGE of PURE GOLD, Singing the Sweetest Notes of the Nightingale and Canary. Two Exquisite Groups of AUTOMATON SINGING BIRDS flying from Branch to Branch! BEAUTIFUL JEWELLED THEATRE. AUTOMATON CONJUROR! TWO MECHANICAL LADIES, SIZE OF LIFE, PLAY DUETS ON FLUTES. SUPERB DISPLAY OF SEVERAL THOUSAND FEET OF SPLENDID NEEDLE WORK TAPESTRY PICTURES. BEAUTIFUL LARGE MODEL OF JERUSALEM, TAKEN ON THE SPOTS 63 WAX MODELS OF KINGS, QUEENS, OTHER ILLUSTRIOUS CHARACTERS. ELEGANT COSMORAMIC VIEWS, OF THE APARTMENTS IN WINDSOR CASTLE, MUSICAL CLOCKS, CHICKEN HATCHING DAILY. Pianoforte by Miss BUTLER, Every Evening Admission to the whole of the Exhibitions, One Shilling — Children Half price. Morning from 11 till 5 Evening. Catalogues 3d. each. J. W. PEEL's Steam Machine, 74, New Cat, Lambeth

The Learned Cats. A handbill advertising performances by Signor Cappelli's famous cats at 248 Regent Street. Printed by J W Peel at New Cut, Lambeth, 1829

Signor Cappelli's, 248 Regent Street is advertised as next-door to the The Argyll Rooms an entertainment venue on Little Argyll Street, Regent Street, London, England.

The rooms were let for miscellaneous performances and exhibitions, such as a French exhibition of dramas performed by puppets, called The French Theatre du Petit Lazary, which was given during the years 1828 and 1829.

In 1829–1830 the rooms were tenanted by Ivan Chabert, calling himself "The Fire King," who entertained the public by placing himself in a heated oven and cooking a steak in it, swallowing phosphorus, and other fiery feats. It was during his tenancy, on the evening of 6 February 1830 that a fire broke out, which in a short time completely destroyed the Argyll Rooms. When it was rebuilt it was mainly replaced by shops.

Chapter Twenty-Six – Mr. Peel's Box Office

At times Mr. Peel's Printing Establishment served as a Box Office. This was not unusual. During the 19th century, the Box Office of a theatre, or circus, was often located in a shop, inn or printer's establishment. An arrangement that might well have increased the number of tickets sold and the money received, as they were open for longer hours. For example, a Poster for Astley's Wonders. Batty's Royal Olympic Circus.

Monday 12 December 1841 declares:

The Box Office under the Direction of Mr. J. W. PEEL, Open Daily from 11 till 4. Mr. BATTY most respectfully solicits Shopkeepers to place this Bill in their Window. All complaints respecting the Non-delivery of the Bills, to be addressed (post-paid) to Mr. BROADFOOT, at the Arena. J. W. PEEL, Printer, 9, New Cut, Lambeth, near the Victoria Theatre

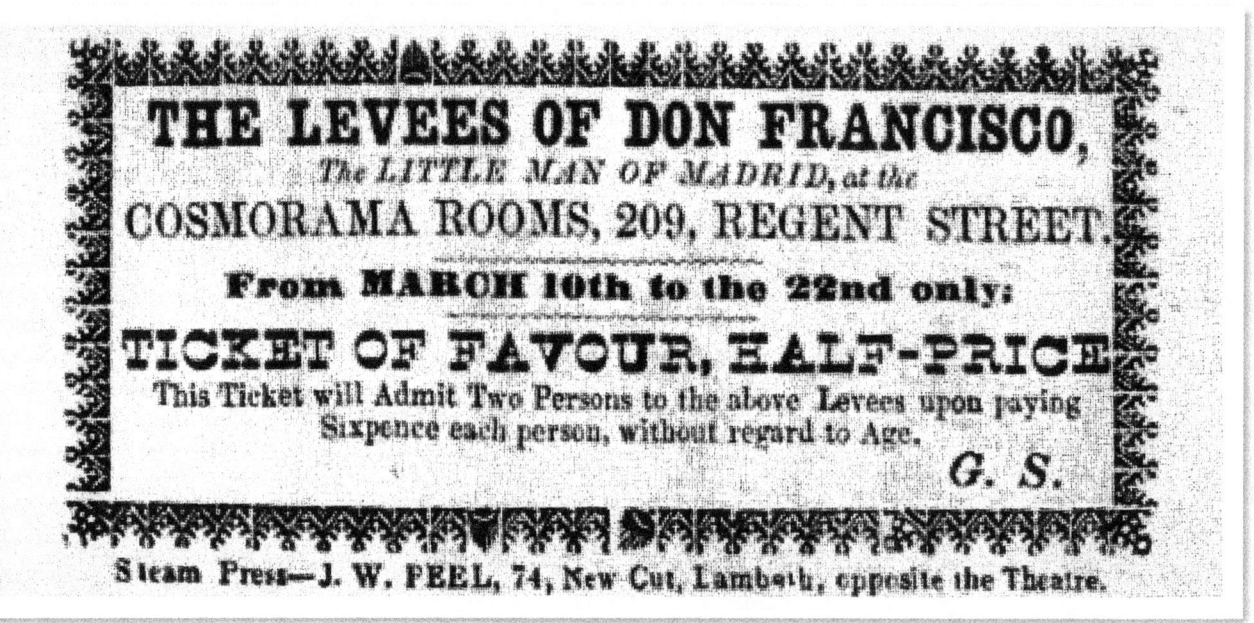

A ticket for The Levees of Don Francisco

A Playbill for Batty's Olympic Circus, National Baths. January 3, 1842 declares that:

The Box Office. Open from 11 till 4 . o' clock Daily, under the Direction of Mr. J. W. Peel, Where Private Boxes and Places may be obtained.

A similar service is promised by the Playbill for Batty's Equestrian Arena. March 7, 1842.

Private Boxes under the Direction of Mr. J. W. Peel.

Mr. Peel was also in charge of the Box Office for his Benefit Night held Batty's Circus Royal on Tuesday March 22, 1842. The poster reads:

Private Boxes under the Direction of Mr. J.W. Peel may be collected Nightly on Application to the Box Office from printer Mr. Peel.

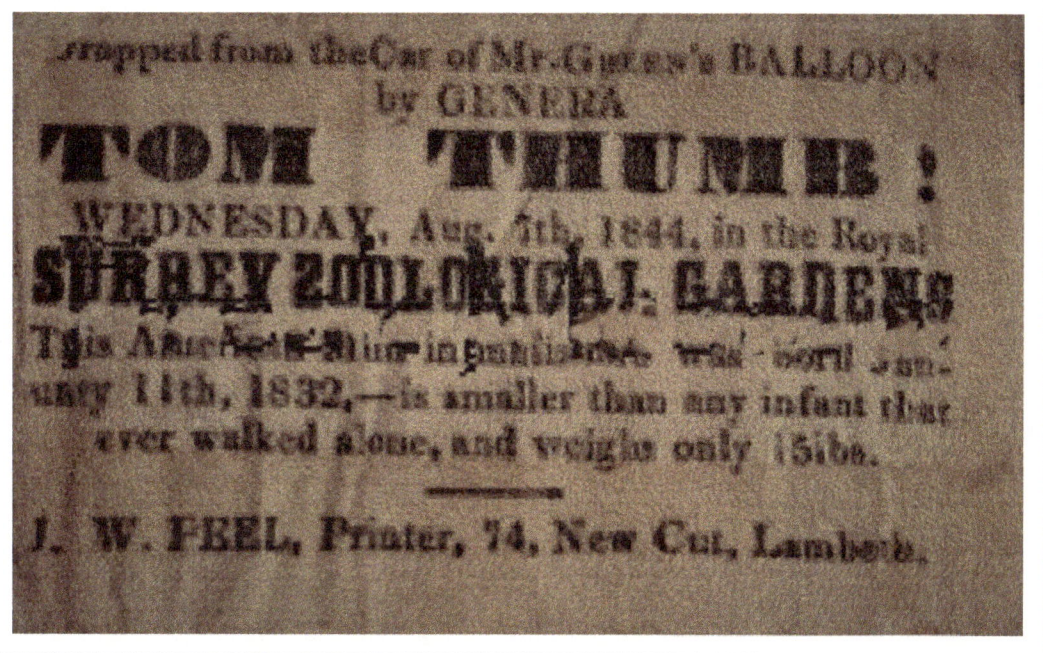

Mr. Peel's Ticket for General Tom Thumb's Appearance

Serving at times as a Box-Office, Mr. Peel was also responsible for printing the tickets. One surviving ticket promotes Tom Thumb. Dropped from the Car of Mr. Green's BALLOON - General. TOM THUMB. Wednesday, August 7th 1844, in the Royal Zoological Gardens. This American Man in Miniature was born January 11th, 1832 - is smaller than any infant that ever walked alone, and weighs only 15 lbs. – J. W. PEEL, 74, New Cut, Lambeth.

Born in Bridgeport, Connecticut, Charles Stratton developed and grew normally for the first six months of his life, at which point he was 25 inches (64 cm) tall and weighed 15 pounds (6.8 kg). Then he suddenly stopped growing.

Phineas T. Barnum, taught the boy how to sing, dance, mime, and impersonate famous people. Then in 1843, Barnum took young Stratton on a tour of Europe, making him an international celebrity. Stratton appeared twice before Queen Victoria.

In 1883, Stratton died unexpectedly of a stroke. He was 45 years old. Over 20,000 people attended the funeral. P. T. Barnum purchased a life-sized statue of Tom Thumb and placed it on top of a column as a grave marker, at Mountain Grove Cemetery in Bridgeport, Connecticut.

Chapter Twenty-Seven – Bridport Hall Prospectus

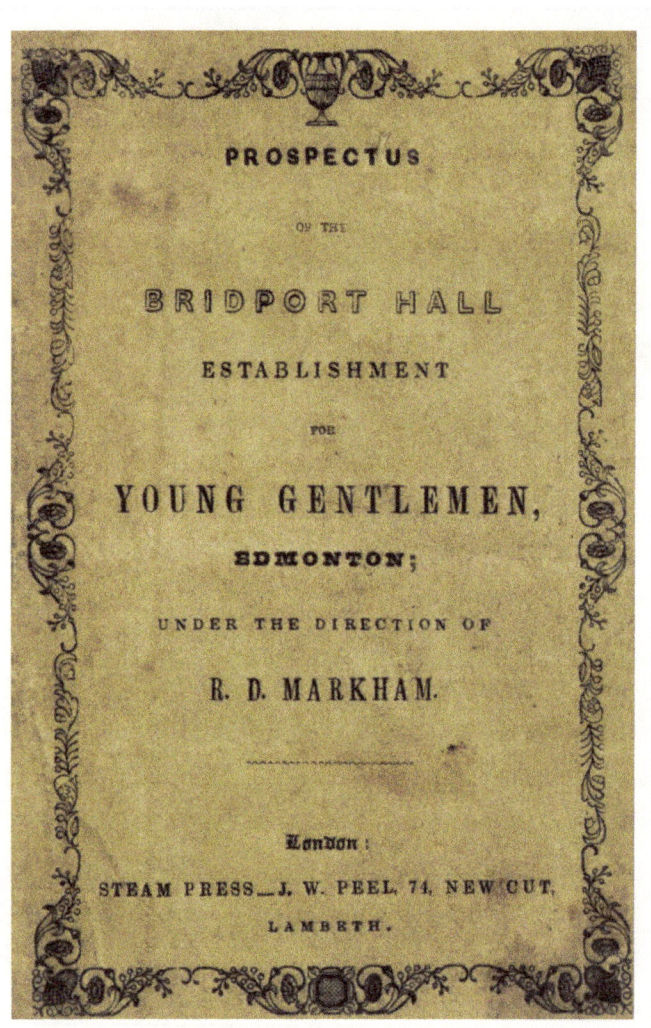

Cover for the Prospectus of the Bridport Hall

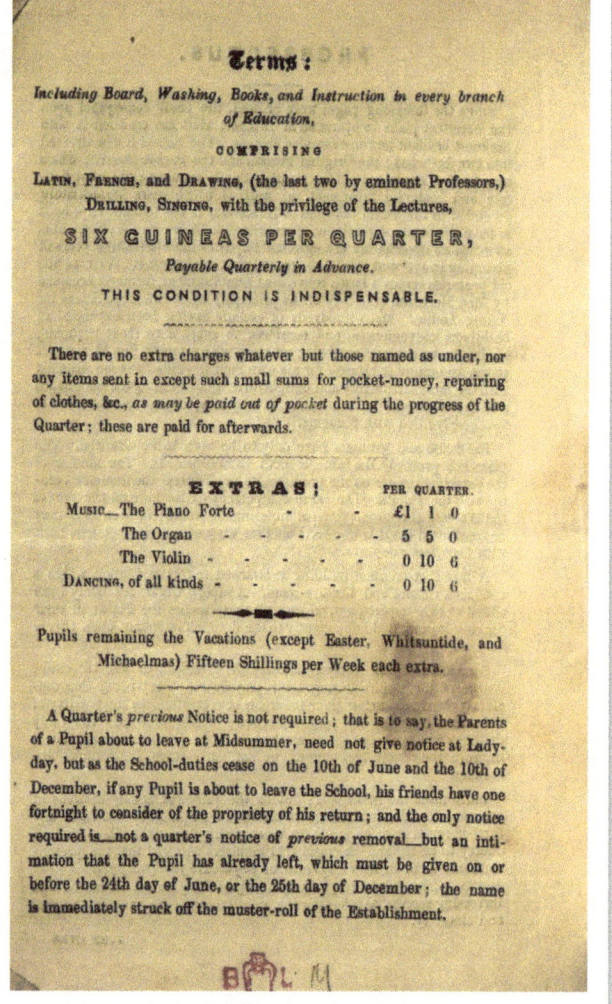

Bridport Hall Terms

From the Prospectus - a Woodcut illustrating Bridport Hall

During the 19th century, especially in its early and middle years, Edmonton was noted for its private schools.

Held at the British Library is a Prospectus of the Bridport Hall establishment for young gentlemen, Edmonton: under the direction of Mr. R.D. Markham ... assisted by duly qualified masters: and the personal superintendence of Mrs. Markham, in the domestic department. Established 1824. Steam Press - Printed by J. W. Peel, 74, New Cut, Lambeth. Published [ca. 1835].

Bridport Hall was a large house which, as the prospectus states, had been opened as a boarding-school in 1824.

The Prospectus gives a complete synopsis of the education system at The Bridport Hall Establishment, Edmonton. Including a map, a wood engraving illustration of the Hall, a detailed description of the lessons taught, and a list of Terms.

With 34 boys attending, it seems Mr. Markham encountered more than his fair share of problems.

At the Old Bailey 10th of September 1840, MICHAEL CARTER, aged 38, was found GUILTY of stealing, 7 spoons, value 3s.; 9 knives, value 6d.; 2 forks, value 6d.; 1 plate, value 1s.; 1 pail, value 1s.; and 2 baskets, value 1d.; the goods of Robert Dallinger Markham.

ROBERT DALLINGER MARKHAM. I keep a school at Bridport Hall, Edmonton. From information I received, I went to the prisoner's lodging, in a cottage which joins my grounds—I found in his bed chamber some spoons and knives and forks, which we had missed a little time before—the prisoner never was in my service in any way—some other articles were found there belonging to my pupils.

Six years later at 2 o'clock on 6 July 1846, The St. James Chronicle records Robert Dallinger Markham of Bridport Hall, Edmonton as a declared Bankrupt.

Chapter Twenty-Eight – Mr. Peel and the Wood Engravers

In the early decades of the 19th century, wood-engravers were in great demand. Master engravers occupied a place in society above humbler compositors, machine minders, and journeymen of the printing trade.

Woodcut illustrations became widely used to enliven the appeal of the Circus Poster. Outsourcing blocks to freelancer wood-engravers was common practice by the middle of the 1800s, but often they were not acknowledged on their work.

During his apprenticeship John Websdale Peel had been taught wood engravers' skills. One woodcut bears his name, and several other illustrations can be attributed to his hand.

In fact the success of Mr. Peel's Posters could, in part, have been due to the skill and artistry of the extremely talented freelance woodcut engravers that he engaged. Supplying Mr. Peel with wonderful elaborate engravings that could only enhance the poster's typographical content. Master wood engravers such as William Clubb, George Dorrington, William Elden Earl and Charles D Laing.

Mr. Peel's Woodcut of Mazappa 6th August 1838

Mr. Peel's Woodcut of Mazappa. Playbill for Astley's Royal Amphitheatre of the Arts. December 22, 1845

It is noticeable that Mr. Peel used his wood engravings many times over the years. The same illustration appearing on different posters. Mr. Peel's poster for Astley's...Mazeppa! And the Wild Horse. Dated 6th August 1838 carries a beautiful wood-engraving by Peel, illustrating Mazeppa's Ride, a constant theme of the equestrian shows.

He uses the same wood block for a Playbill promoting the same show at Astley's Royal Amphitheatre of the Arts on December 22, 1845. And again, on a Playbill for Batty: Astley's Royal Amphitheatre, Westminster Bridge on October 7th, 1850.

Although not signed, many of the wood-engravings that can be attributed to Mr. Peel's hand depict horses. During the trial of WILLIAM HAYLEY at The Old Bailey, on the 30th June 1831. Mr. Peel, cross-examined by MR. ALLEY states: "I go to Ascot races; you may have seen me there." Through his wood-cuts Mr. Peel shows his love of horses, and that he was a very capable draughtsman.

William Clubb

During the same trial of WILLIAM HAYLEY, 30th June 1831 at The Old Bailey. On a charge of Deception: fraud. Mr. Peel refers to the engraver Mr. Clubb.

JURY to J. W. PEEL. Q. "Did you engrave the plate?"

A." No, Mr. Clubb; the name of Ellis was put on it according to the copy; I took the order, and gave it to Clubb to engrave."

It is no wonder that Mr. Peel gave William Clubb the Share Certificates to engrave. Clubb and Son, engravers and printers were capable of the most extraordinary fine work.

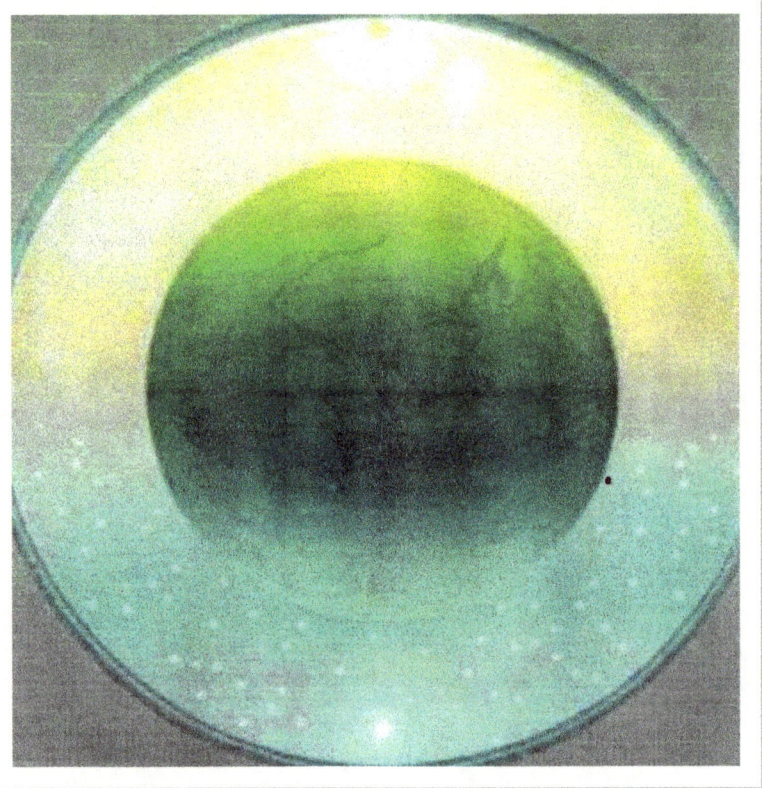

A celestial map - Lodowicke Muggleton

In 1846 they engraved the Muggletonian Astronomical prints.

Engravings that were printed in colour. Six of which were engraved by W P Clubb & Son, 7 Charterhouse Street, London, and printed by George Baxter Patentee, 11, Northampton Square, London.

Muggletonianism was a Protestant sect movement founded in 1651 and named after Lodowicke Muggleton. The celestial maps, published by Isaac Frost, British 1793-1858- in his book Two Systems of Astronomy, illustrate many aspects of the sect's beliefs.

There is a case to be made that William Blake was well aware of the Muggletonians.

George Dorrington

In 1845 George Dorrington was living and working from 143 Blackfriars Road, just around the corner from John Websdale Peel in New Cut.

In the late 1840's Dorrington engraved a number of woodcuts for an edition of The Life and Adventures of Robinson Crusoe, by Daniel Defoe, printed circa 1850. The edition was embellished with three hundred engravings, after designs by J.J. Grandville. London: Willoughby & Co. Grandville's illustrations were initially published in 1840 by H. Fournier aîné, Paris; George Dorrington copied Grandville's woodcuts for this edition. Two of them versions of Grandville's frontispiece, which depicts a monument to Crusoe. One critic, harshly, called Dorrington's engravings for this edition, "mediocre at best".

From June 1855, Dorrington supplied wood engravings to at least eight illustrated weeklies, including, The Illustrated Derbyshire Chronicle, and The St. Neots Chronicle.

Mr Peel's Poster

Dorrington's engraving for Astley's Poster 12th September 1838.

George Dorrington's wood-engravings for Mr. Peel included lions and tigers on the Astley's poster of 12th September 1838, and galloping horses on an Astley's poster of 22nd July 1840.

There is a re-working of Dorrington's wood engraving, for Batty's Olympic Circus on the 17th January 1842 which could possibly be Mr. Peel re-using George Dorrington's original block.

William Elden Earle

Mr. Peel had a lot in common with William Elden Earle. Both men were born in Norwich, Norfolk. William Elden Earle had been baptised in the same church that Mr. Peel's parents married in. They had both made the trip to London; living near each other in Lambeth and both set up businesses, using apprentices.

Re-use of Dorrington's original Print

Victoria Theatre Poster 21st March 1853

William Elden Earle supplied Mr. Peel with high quality wood engravings for his posters. Both Astley's Poster Monday 2 May 1853 and the Victoria Theatre, Monday 21 March 1853 benefitting from William Earle's accomplished woodcuts.

Coloured engravings by W E Earl shows the Nassau balloon, carrying the English aeronaut Charles Green (1785-1870) and six other passengers, ascending from Norwich, Norfolk on Thursday 24 September, 1840. Green used this coal gas-filled balloon for his most famous flight from London to Nassau in Germany in 1836. It was on this voyage, that Green succesfully completed the world's longest flight, at the time, covering an estimated 480 miles (770 km) in 18 hours.

Charles D. Laing

The prolific Charles D. Laing flourished as a wood engraver in London during the mid-eighteen hundreds. In 1851 he was living in Clerkenwell and describes himself as an engraver on wood.

Working in London, Charles Laing produced many fine illustrations. The Wellcome Collection holds a number of his architectural engravings. As does the V & A. The collection forming a substantial part of the W. Harry Rogers Archive. To quote the information on the archive provided by 'RW' on 6 February 1998 on the registered file 1997/1476: 'It is extraordinarily rare to have this kind of documentation at this level of production for the middle decades of the 19th century...'

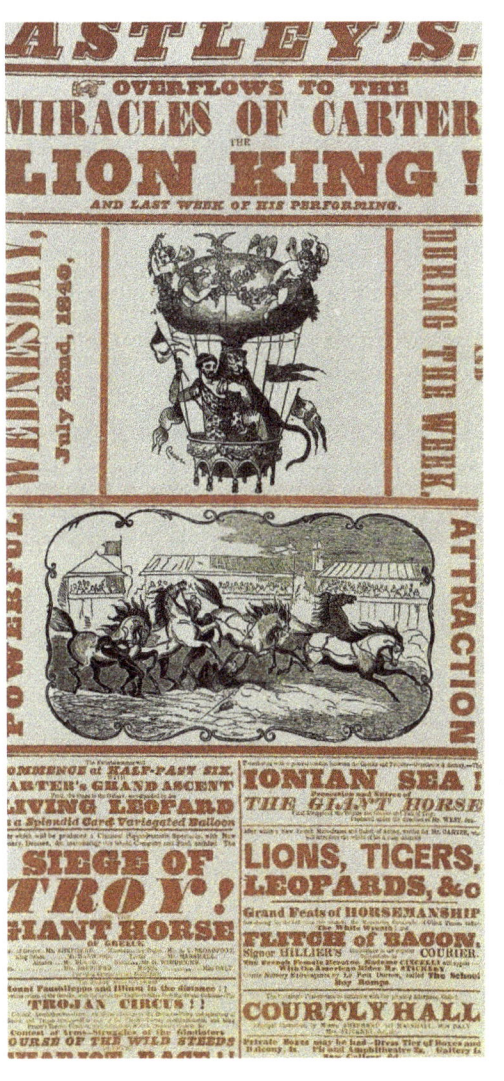

Playbill for Astley's Royal Amphitheatre, July 27, 1840

Balloon Illustration for Astley's poster 1st October 1838

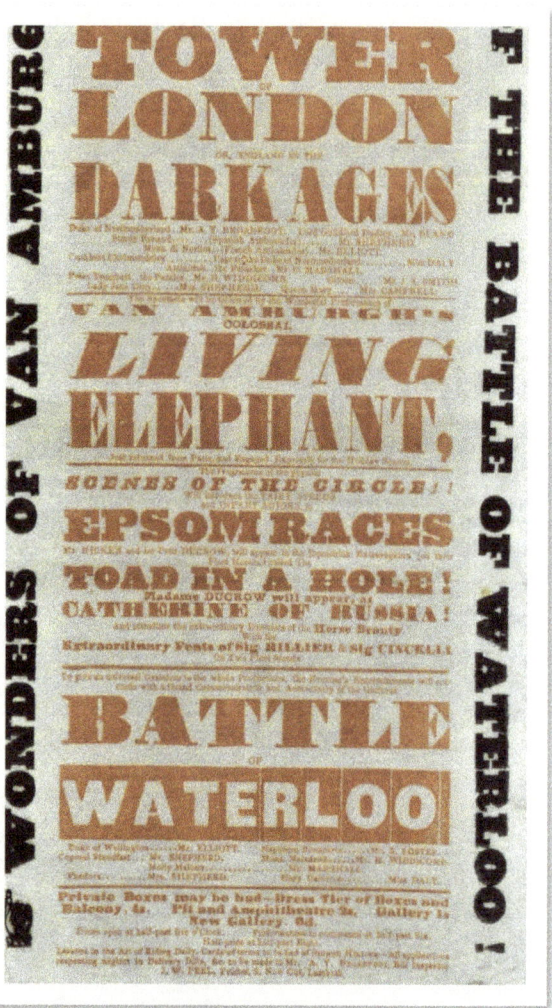

Poster for Astley's
Monday 15th June 1840

Poster for Astley's
Monday 15th June 1840

Laing's work for Mr. Peel includes a Playbill for Astley's Royal Amphitheatre, July 27, 1840.

A beautiful Balloon illustration for an Astley's poster on Monday 1 October 1838; and the Poster for Astley's Monday 15 June 1840, which displays a superbly detailed wood-engraving of the Tower of London.

George Parry Hearder

Living and working as a letterpress printer and wood engraver, in Plymouth, Devon, England. George Parry Hearder's work was used by Mr. Peel on The Cornwall's Royal Circus Poster, dated May 29, 1843. Printer: J. W. Peel - Engraver: Hearder

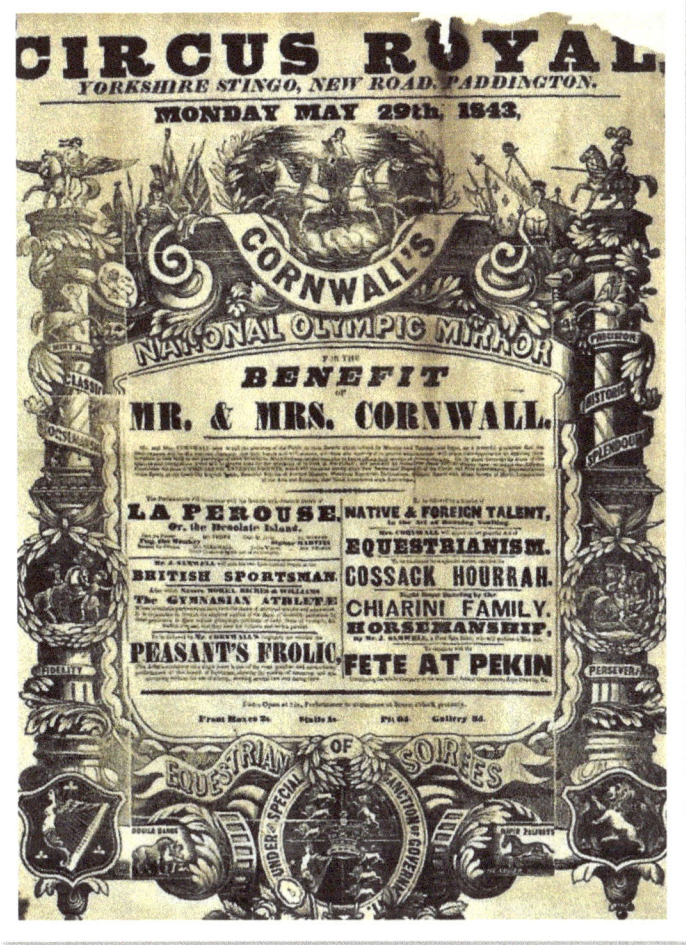
The Cornwall's Royal Circus Poster dated May 29, 1843

Detail of Cornwall's Royal Circus Poster, May 29, 1843

Chapter Twenty-Nine – Mr. Peel the Freemason

Mr. Peel's father had been a Freemason, so it would have been no surprise when, according to the Ledger, John Websdale Peel was initiated into the Constitutional Lodge, London. His Initiation Date is given as the 17th October 1839.

His First Payment Year on Register as 1839. His Profession a Printer.

Mr. Peel kept up his subscription until 1850.

John Websdale Peel - The Constitutional Lodge, London.

Within the Craft of Freemasonry there are three Degrees: Entered Apprentice, Fellow Craft and Master Mason. A man will normally pass through these three degrees, known as initiation, passing and raising, and the date that he passes each degree is recorded in the register. When he has passed the three degrees he then becomes a Master Mason.

Freemasonry became an important part of John Websdale Peel's life. He found that he was able to capture his ideas, and what it meant to him to be a Freemason within the wood engravings he used on the posters.

Poster for Astley's, 27 September 1852

For example: the woodcut, illustrating an Astley's poster of 13 October 1843, and used again in a handbill for Astley's, 27 September 1852, was full of Masonic Symbolism and Imagery. They contained:

An Anchor - Symbol of Hope, Patience and Permanence: A Beehive - Emblem of Industry, and Hard-Work. The Ear of Corn - An expression of Freemasonry and growth: Laurel Wreaths - symbolising Success and victory: Pegusus - Symbol of Vitue and Inspiration: The Lyre - Resonance From a single note, from the symbol to the ritual: and the Incense Pot - Held by the man represents a Pure Heart. The Clouds of rising smoke symbolizing prayers from a pure heart rising up.

1830 Cooke's Circus. Poster

A Poster by John Websdale Peel advertising a performance in 1830. Cooke's circus. A woodcut image shows Mr. Wells, the Antipodean Clown, which explains the use of the upside-down word CLOWN.

This Poster gave Mr. Peel another opportunity to incorporate Masonic symbols into his work: The All Seeing Eye - also known as the Eye of Providence or the Masonic Eye. In Freemasonry, this is a symbol used to remind members that the Great Architect of the Universe; God is observing all deeds, actions, and human thoughts. A Pointing Fore-finger in the poster - the index finger pointing upwards. Symbolizing the hope of heaven, and a "sign of preservation" and faith.

Playbill for Prince & Powell's Circus Royal. July 31, 1843

Price & Powell's Circus poster, for April 13th 1843, invites people to "Go and See Powell drive his Stud of REAL CATS, Four in Hand, several times round the circle."

Similarly, Playbill's for Prince & Powell's Circus Royal, dated 8 May 1843, and July 31, 1843, advertises " Mr. Dewhurst driving his Stud of Real Cats, Four in Hand, several times round the circle. Here we Go, Gallop and Trot: Tibby, Tabby, Toddle and Tot."

Using the same woodcut illustration, these Playbills and posters show a Clown in a four-wheeled chariot being pulled by four cats. His left leg is extended, and he is holding a whip. On the side of the Chariot is the single most, universally recognised, symbol of Freemasonry. The Square and Compass.

Mr. Peel's use of the Square and Compass is an indication of how much being a Freemason meant to him. The square and compasses, the architect's tools, are used in Masonic ritual. They tell of Masonic History, and as emblems teach symbolic lessons. However, it is no coincidence that the language used to advertise these acts is also similar. Both talk of "Four in Hand, several times round the circle". In Freemasonry, the square and circle shapes relate to the problem of "Squaring The Circle," said to be the primary goal of the Masonic craft.

Chapter Thirty – Mr. Peel's Legacy

Mr. Peel died on 6th December 1859. Five years after Mr. Peel's death there was printed a poster that stands as a testament to the influence and high regard with which John Websdale Peel was remembered. It simply reads:

CREMORNE Wednesday July 20th 1864 GODARDS GRAND ASCENT One Shilling

Printed by Nowell's (late Peel's) Steam Machine, 74 New Cut, Lambeth.

Mr. Peel's legacy lived on. People remembered him, and his posters. It could even be argued that some of Mr. Peel's posters contained designs and illustrations far ahead of their time. More in keeping with Twentieth Century Design than the first half of the Nineteenth Century. Compared with the ordinary day to day Victorian illustrations, Mr. Peel's posters introduced woodcuts that were almost revolutionary.

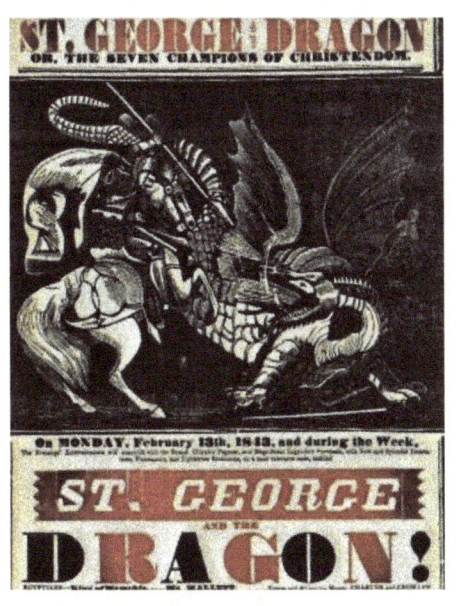

A woodcut from a Playbill for Price & Powell's Circus 1843

Woodcut. George and the Dragon

It is a sobering thought that at the time they were made, more people in London would have been familiar with Mr. Peel's posters than William Blake's graphic work. Even though Blake in the 1820s was living a few streets away from Mr. Peel.

From the 1820s, the sheer output of Mr. Peel's Printing Office, a ready market and the very nature of the places of entertainment that Mr. Peel's Posters promoted, ensured a large audience. For a price, the public were invited to inhabit a fantasy world. By entering a theatre, circus or arena, they were taken to a different world. A world where the past could be recreated, great battles fought, and amazing spectacles witnessed. All a far cry from the grim realities of nineteenth century London. It is no surprise that Charles Dickens himself frequented these 'Dream Palaces'.

Wonders of the Three Olympians, British Museum. Production - 1839

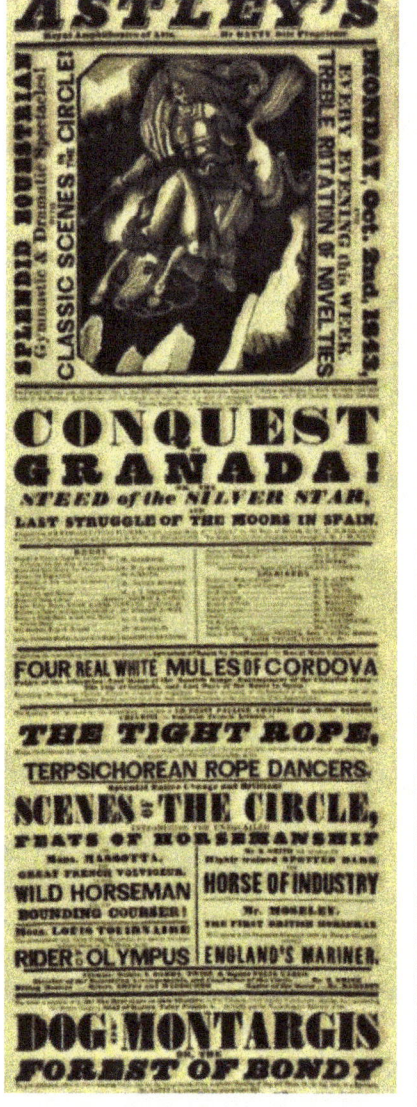

Poster for Astley's October 2nd 1843

Poster for Astley's October 9th 1843

Woodcut for Poster for Astley's October 2nd 1843

Mr. Peel's Posters sold the dream.

For a few hours it was possible to forget day to day problems and hardships. Anyone could be part of this dreamworld if they purchased a ticket.

Mr. Peel inhabited this world. He could walk beside the canal with the stars of Astley's. He was friends with, and worked with the managers of theatres, such as Davidge at the Royal Victoria. He knew his audience, and his posters offered that audience a very different world to their own.

Mr. Peel could also escape. He could escape from the horrors of Death in a Rage, and the deaths of the young in the family he grew up in. The dreams that his posters advertised with their bright words and rich woodcuts were needed. They were needed to recover from the nightmares of everyday living. After all everyone needs the magic of dreams.

Acknowledgements

Telling the story of the life and work of John Websdale Peel would not have been possible without the kind support of the following helpful individuals, and their organisations.

Christian Algar, Curator, Printed Heritage Collections
The British Library, 96 Euston Road, London, NW1 2DB
christian.algar@bl.uk
www.bl.uk

Gerard Greene - Redbridge Museum & Heritage Centre Manager
Redbridge Central Library, Clements Road, Ilford, Essex IG11A
www.redbridge.gov.uk/museum

Elspeth Healey Special Collections Librarian
Kenneth Spencer Research Library
The University of Kansas
1450 Poplar Lane
Lawrence, KS 6604
ehealey@ku.edu

Stella Wisdom
Digital Curator, Contemporary British Collections
96 Euston Road
London
NW1 2DB
digitalresearch@bl.uk

Varun Gupta and his team at White Magic Studios for giving Mr. Peel a wider audience.

I would also like to acknowledge the amazing support of my wife Heather Joy, and my family, during my years of researching, compiling, and telling the story of Mr. Peel.

References

About Freemasonry - United Grand Lodge of England - https://www.ugle.org.uk/about-freemasonry
Ancestry,uk - https://www.ancestry.com/
Alamy Stock Photo - https://www.alamy.com
Arthur Lloyd.co.uk - www.arthurlloyd.co.uk
Biblio - https://biblio.co.uk
British History Online - https://www.british-history.ac.uk/
The British Library - https://www.bl.uk
The British Museum - https://www.britishmuseum.org
Devon History Society - https://www.devonhistorysociety.org.uk
Family Search - https://www.familysearch.org
The Genealogist - https://www.thegenealogist.co.uk
General Register Office (GRO) - Official information on ... - https://www.gro.gov.uk/gro/content
Genuki - https://www.genuki.org.uk
House of Commons Hansard archives - UK Parliament - https://www.parliament.uk/business/publications/hansard/commons
The Harry Ransom Center. Texas - https://www.hrc.utexas.edu/
The Kenneth Spencer Library - https://spencer.lib.ku.edu
Lambeth Archives | Lambeth Council - https://www.lambeth.gov.uk/places/lambeth-archives
London Metropolitan Archives - https://search.lma.gov.uk
Map & Plan Collection Online - mapco.net/london.htm
Newspaper Archives- https://www.britishnewspaperarchive.co.uk
Museum of London - https://www.museumoflondon.org.uk
My Heritage - https://www.myheritage.com
The National Archives - https://www.nationalarchives.gov.uk
The Old Bailey - https://www.oldbaileyonline.org
The Ringling:
(Tibbals Circus Collection) - https://www.ringling.org

Redbridge Museum & Heritage Centre - www.redbridge.gov.uk/museum

Romantic London - A research project by Matthew Sangster ... - www.romanticlondon.org

Science Museum - www.sciencemuseum.org.uk

Local History Library and Archive - Southwark Council - https://www.southwark.gov.uk/libraries/local-history-library-and-archive

Surrey History Centre | The National Archives -https://discovery.nationalarchives.gov.uk

V & A - https://www.vam.ac.uk

Wikipedia - https://www.wikipedia.org

Wikipedia - Commons - https://www.commons.wikimedia.org

Wellcome Collection - wellcomecollection.org

YouTube - https://youtu.be/ZcGWYKg23VA

Further References From:

Christian Algar,

Curator, Printed Heritage Collections

The British Library, 96 Euston Road, London, NW1 2DB

The main point of entry for us when looking at printers is the British Book Trade Index – here's a link to John Websdale Peele's entry http://bbti.bodleian.ox.ac.uk/details/?traderid=53508

Details are trawled from many sources – trade directories, imprints in books and published research – but 'jobbing' printers of bills and posters are not always represented.

There will be printed items in the collection here which are not digitised.....

There are several volumes with Astley's posters in the collection and some are described as being printed by Peele (one by. "J. W. Peel's Steam Machine, 74, New Cut, Lambeth"!)

Title: Astley's under the management of Messrs Ducrow and West, Jun. The extraordinary overflows during the past week, having surpassed the greatest success ever known in the Amphitheatre, the Proprietors, Messrs. Ducrow and West think it to their interest ... to repeat the same unequalled entertainments this present Monday, August 1st, 1836, and every evening during the week. The performance will commence ... with an entirely new equestrian oriental spectacle ... under the title of Lalla Rookh!! or, the Ghebers of the desert! ... In the course of the evening, will be given a new grand Arab spectacle .. under the title of the One hundred battle steeds or the enchanted Arabs! ... The evening's performances to conclude with for the seventh time at this theatre, a new melo-dramatic skech, called The blind orphan or, the 2 dogs of Ravensdale. The two dogs, by Carlo & Neptune ...

Author: Astley's Amphitheatre.

Contributor: John Fillinham former owner.

Other Titles: Variant Title: Lalla Rookh, or the Gherbers of the desert

Variant Title: One hundred battle steeds of the enchanted Arabs

Variant Title: Blind orphan or the 2 dogs of Ravensdale

Subjects: Circus animals; Broadsides -- Great Britain -- 19th century; Advertising -- Circus -- Great Britain -- 19th century

Publication Details: [London] : J. W. Peel, Printer, Lambeth, [1836.]

Language: English

Identifier: System number 015491861

Notes: Poster advertsising equestrian performances at Astley's on Monday, August 1st, 1836, in which the trained horses of Mr. Ducrow take part in a 'grand pageant' entitled 'The Royal Falconers', and in a grand oriental spectacle showing 'games of one hundred mounted warriors' and 'pyramids of men & horses 30 ft. high'.

Physical Description: 1 sheet ([1] p.) ; 49 x 25 cm.

Copy Note: Ownership: Copy at 1889.b.10/6(51). Included in the Fillinham Collection (VI. Trained Animals, Menageries, etc).

Shelfmark(s): General Reference Collection 1889.b.10/6(51) UIN: BLL01015491861

Title: Astley's Royal Amphitheatre ... Immense success of the new sporting hippo-drama! ... in two acts, written expressly for this Theatre, by Mr. W. E. Suter, illustrating the phases of a "sporting man's career," produced with new scenery, costumes, and appointments, and entitled The Chase or, life on the turf! ... To be followed by an unprecedented display of equestrian and gymnastic scenes of the arena introducing Mr. W. Cooke's highly-trained horses and ponies...

Author: Astley's Amphitheatre.

Contributor: John Fillinham former owner.

Subjects: Circus animals; Broadsides -- Great Britain -- 19th century; Advertising -- Theatre -- Great Britain -- 19th century

Publication Details: [London] : J. W. Peel's Steam Machine, 74, New Cut, Lambeth, [1853.]

Language: English

Identifier: System number 015513808

Notes: Poster advertising a performance at Astley's on June 6, 1853, which will include 'fox chase with real fox and pack of hounds' and 'Aylesbury leap of a horse over a dining table'.

Physical Description: 1 sheet ([1p.]) ; 37 x 11 cm.

Copy Note: Ownership: Copy at 1889.b.10/6(98). Included in the Fillinham Collection (VI. Trained Animals, Menageries, etc). MS. date on poster (in John Fillinham's hand): June 6, 1853.

Shelfmark(s): General Reference Collection 1889.b.10/6(98)
UIN: BLL01015513808

Title: [A collection of playbills for Astley's Royal Amphitheatre for the years 1821-1845.]

Author: Astley's Royal Amphitheatre (LONDON)

Publication Details: [London], [1821, 45]

Identifier: System number: 002220293

Notes: The series is not complete.

Physical Description: (folio)

Shelfmark(s): General Reference Collection Playbills.171. UIN: BLL01002220293

Title: A collection of playbills from Astley's Amphitheatre 1850-1858.
Author: Astley's Amphitheatre.
Subjects: Theater -- Great Britain -- 19th Century
Publication Details: [London : s.n.], 1850-1858.
Language: English
Identifier: System number 015326087
Physical Description: 3 v. (151, 160, 155 sheets) ; 53 cm.
Holdings Notes: General Reference Collection Playbills 173 [Bound in 3 volumes]
Shelfmark(s): General Reference Collection Playbills 173 UIN: BLL01015326087

There are a handful of items in the collection which are specified as printed by Peele; three have been digitised so you can look at those online. The shelfmarks are given below. You can find the records on the Library's catalogue http://explore.bl.uk/ using the sheflmarks stripped of all punctuation (ie RB23a12922):

General Reference Collection Digital Store RB.23.a.12922 DRT
General Reference Collection Digital Store 8247.bbb.41. DRT
General Reference Collection Digital Store 1153.l.5. DRT
General Reference Collection 1889.b.10/6(32a)
General Reference Collection 1889.b.10/6(51)
General Reference Collection 1889.b.10/6(44)
General Reference Collection 1889.b.10/6(27)
General Reference Collection 1889.b.10/6(49)
General Reference Collection 10351.dd.9.(3.)
General Reference Collection RB.23.b.4336(13)
General Reference Collection 1889.b.10/6(98)
General Reference Collection 1889.b.10/6(47)

Further From:
Elspeth Healey
Special Collections Librarian
Kenneth Spencer Research Library
University of Kansas

RE: John Websdale Peel's posters for Astley's Amphitheatre...ours are included in a three-volume scrapbook devoted to Astley's Amphitheatre. Unfortunately, the page-by-page contents of the scrapbook have not been inventoried, so alas I'm not able to provide a more detailed listing.

...I especially enjoyed seeing the circus posters at https://peels.omeka.net/exhibits/show/astley-s-posters/astley-s-circus-collection-her, many of which we have copies of in our Astley's Amphitheatre scrapbooks.

www.ingramcontent.com/pod-product-compliance
Lightning Source LLC
Chambersburg PA
CBHW051254110526
44588CB00026B/2987